WOVEN

Angie Smith

WOVEN

Understanding the Bible as
One *Seamless* Story

B&H
PUBLISHING
NASHVILLE, TENNESSEE

978-1-4627-9660-1

Published by B&H Publishing Group
Nashville, Tennessee

Dewey Decimal Classification: 220.07
Subject Heading: BIBLE—STUDY AND TEACHING / BIBLE—
CHRONOLOGY / BIBLE—READING

Cover design by B&H Publishing Group. Macramé by Karele
Bellavance/BohoMontreal. Cover photo by Randy Hughes.
Brick texture by Nataliya Sdobnikova/shutterstock. Interior
images of Tabernacle of Moses and Ark of Covenant © Maryna
Kriuchenko | Dreamstime.com. Author photo by Abby Smith.

It is the Publisher's goal to minimize disruption caused by
technical errors or invalid websites. While all links are active
at the time of publication, because of the dynamic nature of the
internet, some web addresses or links contained in this book
may have changed and may no longer be valid. B&H Publishing
Group bears no responsibility for the continuity or content of
the external site, nor for that of subsequent links. Contact the
external site for answers to questions regarding its content.

2 3 4 5 6 7 8 • 25 24 23 22 21

For Jenn, who decided to follow Jesus and taught me more than I will ever be able to teach anyone else. J, you're everything your big sister wants to be, and I love you more than you'll ever know.

CONTENTS

INTRODUCTION

The Bible.

Holy Bible.

All those pages.

Such thin, thin pages.

For many years of my life, that's kind of all the Bible seemed to be to me. To be honest, I didn't give it a ton of thought for the majority of that time. I wasn't raised in a Christian home, and I never had a desire to learn more about Scripture. I knew enough to know the Bible was important, of course—knew it was certainly important to all those grandmas and good girls and other Jesus-people who carried it with them so faithfully to church each week.

I have vivid memories of the sweet family who took me to church with them for several Sundays. I remember the pews and the holy silence there. It was intriguing to me because I did feel something that I couldn't quite put into words. I think there are a million ways a person can feel a tug toward faith and not know what to do with it.

I also went because I loved the smell of the leather in their Volvo and the sound of Bach blasting around me.

But I could never understand those crisp, crinkly Bible pages. They taunted me. *Taunting tissue.* That's what the Bible felt like.

And I hated that. Because I'm a pretty bright person. I tend to pick up on things fairly quickly, can usually get my mind wrapped around stuff—even complicated stuff— if I'm curious enough about it and committed enough to figuring it out. But the Bible was just different. I couldn't make any sense of it. Even after I really *wanted* to make sense of it. It was frustrating.

What I've found out in the years since, however, is that . . . here, I'll whisper it to you: *we all kind of feel that way, don't we?*

If you said no, I'm going to go ahead and ask you to look for something else to read, because I don't think you're being honest with me. We *all* struggle to understand the Bible. You know we do.

That's because the Bible is unlike any other book in all the world. Part of the reason for this—and we wouldn't know it simply by looking at it—is that the Bible is not just a book. It's a library of books. It's made up of historical accounts and spiritual instruction and handwritten letters and—just some outright beautiful writing—prophecy, poetry, praise songs, personal conversations. Each book of the Bible gives us deeper, additional insights into what God was saying or doing with his people during specific points along the time line. And while a lot of it does read like a continuously running narrative, with page after page of an ongoing story arc that you can track and trace and follow along with, other parts of it are there for different reasons than that.

Some of the books, for instance, like Ruth and Esther, break off to tell a single, isolated story. Others, like the books of Old Testament prophecy or the letters of Paul, sort of telescope outward from parts of the story that are told elsewhere.

[Side note to you: if you've never heard of Ruth or the Old Testament or Paul or anything else you just read, I am SO EXCITED you're here. You're going to look back to this page when you're done and say with a laugh, "Who doesn't know the background story of Paul and why it's such a spectacular example of the gospel?" Promise.]

One particular book, in fact—the book of Job—which appears near the middle of the Bible (pronounced JOBE, not JOB), dates all the way back toward the beginning, more like where Genesis is. Yes, you read that correctly.

So, I may as well break the news to you now in case you need some time to process it.

The books of the Bible are not entirely in order.

I know. It complicates things. When you're reading, you can't always assume the next book is automatically the next thing that happened chronologically.

The reason I mention it up front here is only because if you've ever felt as overwhelmed as I did when I first tried piecing the Bible together . . . *don't*. Who is up to the task of reading a sixty-six-volume set (of anything!) and keeping up with all the information, all the characters' lives, getting all the details down right, and synthesizing it perfectly? Without any help?

And yet even as a collection of more than five dozen books featuring various types of literature, written by forty authors spanning sixteen hundred years, this Book is actually—drumroll!—the telling of *one single story*. We will see Jesus woven (yes, intended) throughout every single bit of it. And that's the part some people have missed about the Bible and about *him*. (I know I had.) He shows up in places we never knew to look.

The Bible has the distinct honor of being the only book that is alive. Sounds strange, I know, but it's true. It is active. It *pierces* us. In case you want to double-check me, that's what the Bible actually says about itself. You'll find it in the book of Hebrews. Which is also not exactly placed in the right order chronolo . . .

Too soon?

Don't panic.

The only important thing to remember right now—and I promise we're going to keep it this simple all the

3

way through—is that God is the one who's telling this story. He's the one who *wrote* this story. He's the one who started *living* this story and who chose to put it into words for us so that we could hear it straight from his mouth, and could keep hearing it, over and over and over and over again.

But we don't want to miss the bigger picture, and the only way we can see it is to pull back the lens.

You may not know one single piece of Scripture. That's okay. You're welcome to hang out here, and I give you my word you're going to be impressed with yourself as you read. Or maybe you've written a dissertation on the different viewpoints of the rapture and you've memorized three-quarters of the Bible. I hope you get something out of this book as well, even if it's just an appreciation for the fonts and the cool maps. Everyone loves the maps (or learns to).

I assure you I'm not going to continue saying it this way throughout all the coming chapters, but I need to say it again right here: God has *woven* himself into his Word and into his people, and the best way for us to follow that thread is to begin tugging on it.

So how do we do that?

Maybe the dissertation lady would like to jump in here.

But truth be told, you've already got everything you need for understanding it. And I'm truly, deeply grateful that you're here. It's the most amazing story. And you ARE going to understand it.

So go ahead and crease the corner of this page. And when you finish the book, I want you to flip back and see if I kept my promise. Feel free to write me nasty emails if you feel like I didn't. I have an amazing assistant, and I will never see them.

But in all seriousness, I'm praying for you right this second.

I know you're going to love the way the Bible is woven together.

Sorry. I had to.

Chapter 1

THE TIME I SCARED LITTLE KIDS' PARENTS

I was in my early twenties when a couple of new friends invited me to a Bible study. I didn't have a clue what that was, but it sounded equal parts intriguing and horrifying, so I agreed to go.

I didn't think of myself as stupid. I was actually in grad school at the time and was the kind of person who didn't give up on anything until I completely understood it. I held impressive college degrees, had published my own academic papers, and was on full scholarship to one of the most prestigious schools in the country—all at the ripe young age of twenty-three. (As writers, we have editors who sometimes add in sentences that make us sound more exciting than we are. Which is why I left in that last one.)

All I needed to do, these girls told me, was go down to the local Christian bookstore and buy a copy of some workbook that we were going to be covering. Sounded simple enough.

So, one day after classes, I drove downtown and found the place. But I realized fairly quickly that this was the kind of parking lot where you turn down the sound of the Beastie Boys when you pull in. I took one look at the posters and the window displays and saw that these were not my people. So I left.

Still, I went to the Bible study anyway, sans workbook. Wasn't a problem. The leader was the kind of southern girl who didn't show up without extra snacks and workbooks. So we all sat on the floor, and I marveled at the whole awkward scene. The lady on the video we were watching would say something like, "Turn to Isaiah, chapter fifty-three," and all fifteen of the other girls opened their Bibles to that exact page simultaneously. Or at least I'm pretty sure I'm remembering that correctly. So, all over again, it was like I was back in that store parking lot, on the outside looking in, wondering how a girl with my past and my problems and my obvious lack of experience with how Bible studies operate was going to make it through the rest of the evening, much less several more weeks of this business, which I'd been told would be the expected time frame.

But I was determined to stick with it. I'm Italian. I had my workbook now. I kind of understood the order of stuff (prayer, talking, snacks, video, more talking, more snacks, more prayer, etc.). So between that night and the time of the next week's meeting, I dug out the only copy of the Bible I owned. (Laugh at your discretion. It was a "Precious Moments" edition.) I spent about an hour and a half attaching sticky notes inside it, marking the pages where the workbook said we'd be looking up Bible verses during the upcoming session.

Ha! I *had* this.

The visual of me walking into that Bible study after a class on applied linear statistical models still makes me laugh. (Yes, that was the name of a real class, and I was the teaching assistant. God bless those kids. I basically showed up with cute hair and acted like I knew what I was doing. This particular strategy has always served me well.) But, oh, sweet little Angie—you really thought you could pull the same tricks with Christianity, didn't you?

That's how it went. Week after week. I planned on adding it to my résumé of adventures and education.

What I *didn't* plan on was falling in love with Jesus.

But the nerd in me is never too far away, so I did what any logical person would do. Except not at all. *I braved the bookstore.* Only I didn't run straight to the four-inch-thick books the way I would've done if I was investigating most other subjects. Instead, I went and sat crisscross-applesauce in the kids' area and pulled out Bibles written for four-year-olds, right there with the stuffed vegetables that were entertaining the (other?) kids around me.

And despite the fact that a few moms were probably keeping a closer eye on their kids than they'd been doing before I got there, it was actually a roaring success. I even *bought* a couple of those Bible storybooks. And, I swear, I'll never forget the indescribably sweet season of time that followed, when I'd come home to my little apartment after school each day, head out on my balcony, open up those brightly colored Bibles, and read the amazing stories someone had rewritten for the children in their life.

All of a sudden, I realized there was a story in the Bible.

I know—and, again, God bless those sweet college students. I'm sorry their parents paid 1903758302 dollars for them to go to Vanderbilt and learn about the importance of applying texturing spray before flat ironing.

Up until then, for example, I'd hear a story about, oh . . . Samson, let's say. Samson and Delilah. I remember knowing that Delilah was bad. No clue where I learned it. I also knew the same about Jezebel. I did not know Jezebel would be eaten by dogs later, but that's for another book. I knew some of these names, but I didn't have any idea where they fell in the story of Scripture. Samson was super-strong, maybe not the brightest guy, whose girlfriend tricked him into letting her cut his hair because she knew he would lose all his power until it grew back, and she stood to make a killing in bribe money if she could pull it off. That's a good one. Who knew his hair would grow back and he'd end up pushing down the main supporting beams of a big building one day with his bare hands and kill a bunch of people, himself included. The little kids' books naturally didn't go into great detail on all of this, but . . .

Okay, I would think, when I'd come across Samson in my Bible now, or in a teaching that I'd heard. *Samson goes HERE . . . in the book of Judges . . . and the judges came between the time of JOSHUA (when Israel entered the Promised Land) and SAMUEL (the last judge), who ushered in the first Israelite kings, Saul and David.*

Samson, Samuel, Joshua, King Saul—they stopped being for me these disembodied names who just floated around somewhere inside my rough, raw-data knowledge base of the Bible. Slowly but surely, I started growing in my ability to pin the stories, events, and details of their lives into the spots they actually occupied in Scripture.

And from there, anchored around those pins, I could start to draw lines tying them together. And the more lines I drew—between more and more of these happenings and sayings and key moments that stood out to me from the Bible—all those loose, straggly threads of connection began to flatten out for me, weaving themselves (oh, my gosh, I cannot stop—is there a hotline for this sort of thing?), yes, *weaving* themselves around each other.

That's when I saw it. It was *all one story.* It is *all one story.* Sixty-six books, and yet *all one story.*

I still can't quite describe for you how empowering this discovery felt to me, and feels to me even now. By no means did I turn into an overnight Bible scholar. In an unexpected turn of events, I am still not a Bible scholar. But I act confident, and that helps.

So here we go.

Couple of things first, by way of caveat: (1) *We won't be covering everything.* What we're embarking on here is a flyover. We'll be picking out the big landmarks of the Bible together, as well as the significant pathways and patterns that run between them. And while we'll hover over several important points to take a closer look, the main purpose of this journey is to get the general lay of the land. By the time we touch down again at the end of these pages, you'll walk away with an insider's awareness on the grand story of Scripture. You'll have seen it with your own eyes.

Also, (2) *We won't be solving every theological question.* Maybe that'll be the next book you read. Maybe you'll jump from here into exploring a particular theme or doctrine from the Bible, wanting to find out how someone else interprets it. Bright, well-intentioned believers can come to various conclusions on a lot of different things, as you know, and God gives us plenty of leeway to seek him together despite our areas of healthy debate. But we won't be doing any debating in this book. Not that I don't have my own reasoned, prayerful opinions on stuff, but the main thing I'm praying for on this trip is for clear skies. If we clog it up with extra baggage, with distracting sidebar arguments, we'll never get there.

And this time, friend, *we're getting there.* Wherever you've felt the need to cover for your lack of biblical fluency, whether real or self-perceived, those days are now coming to a quick and confident end. Granted, you'll never know everything there is to know. We weren't created with the capability for articulating all the mysteries of God. But the Author of this story didn't write it for only a handful of experts to understand while it baffles the rest of us. He wrote it for you, and for me, knowing that he created us to understand it with no need for commentaries and seminars. Those are great, but those are extras.

So why aren't we looking at Genesis yet, Angie?

Hang on. We're close.

It's because I really do have a couple more important things to say at the outset.

First, remember the Bible is real. Now I know you knew that, but because we rightly use the language of "story" to talk about what's written in Scripture, the temptation at least exists to treat it as mere literature or as some sort of mythology. And I want to dismiss that thought entirely, even in how you approach this little book I've written *about* the Bible.

Second, read it with the end in mind. I'm assuming at this point that the biblical roadmap feels a bit fuzzy and disjointed for you. That's okay. That's why we're here. But at the end of this chapter, I've included a two-page, nicely designed layout of the seamless story line of Scripture. And I encourage you to keep turning to it, all along the way. Familiarize yourself with it. Know where we're going.

It's not cheating.

Because when we start, we'll be hitting a lot of huge, foundational events and concepts right out of the gate, and they'll require a few pages to explain. So it'll take us a little while to ramp up before we start to feel like we're making much progress. It might seem slow, but I assure you I have a plan. And part of the reason we won't bog down is because, when we're talking about Adam and Eve, for example, we won't just be talking about Adam and Eve. We won't merely be dealing with the early chapters of Genesis. We'll already be looking ahead, weaving them (my editor added this one; I take zero responsibility) into the much larger story of the Bible—how God, in his love for humankind, chose to deal with this rupture in relationship that Adam and Eve began, and how the rest of the Bible is the telling of that story.

So keep a second bookmark between those pages I mentioned, where I've included all the spoilers. And rather than hanging back as you're reading and letting yourself be surprised by what's next, choose to be surprised instead by how quickly God is strengthening your grasp on the whole Bible—all because you're reading it with the end in mind, even from the start.

Throughout this book, as often as possible, I'll make comments as to how whatever part of the Bible we're studying connects with something that's still centuries down the biblical road. That's because the more time you and I spend becoming articulate with the big picture, the more color and detail we'll see in every picture.

You'll often notice, too, that when I quote directly from Scripture, I will mention the verse I'm referring to. Don't be intimidated by that, if it's something new to you. Don't get worried if you have no clue what they mean. You will.

Lastly, pray. You may have never even tried to pray before, or you may be a pastor's kid who prayed before you learned to talk. Either way, you can ask God to give you supernatural understanding, to fill you with a new joy and delight in his Word. Pray that he will make things clear to you in a way you've possibly never seen in the Scriptures before. Tell him you truly want to know this story, not so that you can more confidently hold your own in Sunday school or Bible study, but—as I said before—simply because you want to know him.

My prayer for you is that, like me, you'll experience your own version of my balcony moments without having to sit in the kids' section of the bookstore. (Though, of course, you should still go to bookstores.) They are magical to me. Bookstores have always been my safe place. I go there when I'm sad, when I'm curious, when I just need to take a break and breathe. Books are the love of my life. Stories are what have held me together.

That's why I can tell you, with much more confidence than I had when teaching classes I could barely pronounce, that all stories have an arc. There's the beginning, the rising action, the climax, and the eventual resolution. In order to model that structure, many of them start with those four classic words, "Once upon a time . . ." But my absolute favorite story, written by the inspiration of my favorite Author, opens with only three:

In the beginning . . .

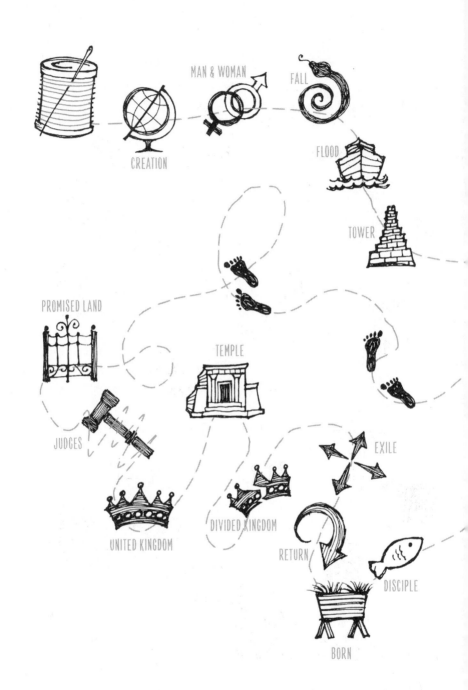

CREATION

MAN & WOMAN

FALL

FLOOD

TOWER

PROMISED LAND

TEMPLE

JUDGES

EXILE

UNITED KINGDOM

DIVIDED KINGDOM

RETURN

DISCIPLE

BORN

Chapter 2

THAT'S GOOD—
NO, THAT'S BAD
Creation and Fall

 It's the perfect start, really.

No. Seriously. Take any of those rare, special moments in life when you've sat back smiling, sighing, gazing contentedly at your immediate surroundings—maybe that clear blue day on the lake, or that crisp fall evening under an amber sunset, or those couple of hours with your family on that one particular Christmas morning—a time when you vividly recall whispering under your breath, *This is perfect.*

I have a lot of those. The first that comes to mind is lying beside my younger sister on a black and yellow raft while our dad pulled us through and across the ocean waves, over and over. The sand stayed scratchy on my arms, and my sister laughed so hard that she almost tipped us over. My dad was wearing a white T-shirt, and it was soaked through where I could see the medallion of Mary around his neck—the one he never took off. I knew that after a while, when the sun started falling, we'd head back to our condo and dress for dinner, all of us a little more sun-kissed than we'd intended to be.

I can feel that memory in a place too deep for words.

That moment, and a million other moments, feel perfect—like there wasn't a single other thing that could've made them better. They're the kinds of memories you try to wrap your arms around, forcing them to stay put or last forever, but you never can.

And there's a reason for that.

We can't experience perfection here. We can have fleeting moments when it *seems* like everything is right in the world, but the truth is, it hasn't been that way since Adam and Eve, and it won't be that way again for a long time. God says he will one day give his people "a new heaven and a new earth" (Rev. 21:1). Until then, we're just trucking through the hard days, asking God to make them joyful days, anticipating the good days.

But, see, that's how the ending helps us process the beginning. If you want to put your finger on all the angst and anger and turmoil and depression that you feel in society around you, and often feel in the heart within you, it springs from being confined to living in a world that hasn't been what it ought to be since Genesis 1 and 2. The fact that nothing's ever really been capable of being or staying "good" (to borrow God's favorite Creation word)—no matter how hard we try or how badly we want it to be—is enough to make us want to curl up in a ball. Or lash out in frustration. Or think we might actually prefer dying to living.

So, the Creation is a not just a story. It's a promise. It's a peek. It's a historical, yet hopeful and forward-looking portrait of everything you'd expect an unlimited, all-powerful God to make when he set out to create an entirely new universe. He took one look at "everything that he had made, and behold, it was very good" (Gen. 1:31)—weighty words from Someone whose standard of goodness, we'll come to see, is purest perfection.

That's where the Bible story begins.

Not that God had a beginning. He's always been there. He has always existed as Father, Son, and Holy Spirit, which is called the Trinity—a super-easy concept that everyone (I mean, NO ONE) totally understands. So, God

(a) has been alive for a literal eternity, (b) exists as three divine Persons, revealed to us as Father, Son, and Spirit, yet (c) is still a united *one* in his essence.

And here's where I'll throw out something that will serve you well as you go through this book and as you study the Word. There are many, many things that you will learn, and they will be mysteries to you because they're intended to be. This doesn't mean they aren't true. *They are.* It just means our brains can't fully comprehend the ways of God. So, we aren't going to be able to know everything. This is not my favorite part of faith. Where are the graphs? Where are the highlighters? I'd pull an all-nighter to understand the "three-in-oneness" of God. I'd buy a Trapper Keeper and tabs. I so wish it worked that way. I could live in the organizational aisles.

But we do know this much: God made us in his image (Gen. 1:27).

We also know this: he was not required to do any of it. Nothing in Scripture indicates that God was bored or restless or was suffering from any lack of fellowship, and therefore we human beings became something "good" for him to have around, as if he needed us as much as we needed him. Internally within the Trinity, God has always enjoyed the highest and best experience of community and fellowship possible, without need of anything external to make things "better" for him. The Father, Son, and Spirit have been hanging out together forever, in a perfect bond of love and unity and relational happiness.

In this way, God doesn't need us, and that's what makes it beautiful. He *chose* to make us. Because he wanted to. To show his glory.

God created the first humans, whom he surrounded with complete, abundant provision and beauty, so that we could experience personal, intimate relationship with him, with the eternal God himself. Or as author Anne Lamott says, "God created us because he thought we would like it."[1] In short, God wanted to share all that love and unity and relational happiness going on between Father, Son, and Spirit *with us*. Pretty amazing, that he would love us that much.

And he kicked it all off with two people you may have heard of.

First, of course, there's *Adam*. "The LORD God formed the man of dust from the ground and breathed into his nostrils the breath of life, and the man became a living creature" (Gen. 2:7). Then there's *Eve*. God wanted Adam to have someone as his companion, someone who was formed in the same way as he was, so that he could share his life with another person. God "caused a deep sleep to fall upon the man, and while he slept took one of his ribs" and somehow used it to create the first woman (Gen. 2:21–22). Every time I read that, I think of a friend of ours who has a clever tattoo on his rib cage devoted to his wife, which says, "You owe me one."

Anyway, Adam's new wife definitely brought some issues into the marriage: namely, the fact that she wasn't a hundred percent sure she could trust this God who'd put them here. And "here," by the way, was a paradise called the garden of Eden, which simply could not have been a more ideal place for launching out in life. Talk about starting at the top. Lush, green, rich, succulent. No leaky faucets or loud neighbors or Tuesday nights at the Laundromat. Nothing but new possibilities with every sunrise, and fresh fruit growing on every tree.

And all of it was freely available to them. All but the fruit from one single tree: "the tree of the knowledge of good and evil" (Gen. 2:17). And the only reason God warned them to stay away from that tree was, again, because of how much he loved them: "For in the day that you eat of it," he said, "you shall surely die" (v. 17b). That's what a loving parent does, right? "See that plant, babe? Don't touch it. It's called poison ivy, and it's not your friend." If I wasn't lovingly interested in preventing my children such torment, I wouldn't even tell them what poison ivy looked like. That's why God warned them.

FALL IN THE GARDEN

Writing in the early 1960s, pastor and author A. W. Tozer said, "What comes into our minds when we think about God is the most important thing about us."[2] That statement always stops me cold. What *does* come into my mind when I think about God? What about you? How do *you* think of him?

Do you think of him as loving? As trustworthy? Is he *for* you? Does he have your best interests in mind? Questions like these, believe it or not, were already swirling, even amid the gentle breezes of Eden. And in Genesis 3, we find out they were prodded by Satan himself, who made his first biblical appearance in verse 1, in the form of (what else) a snake. He shimmied into the picture and put the question to Eve directly:

> "Did God actually say, 'You shall not eat of any tree in the garden'?" (v. 1)

Please note that this is not at all what God said. The garden was *full* of trees he had given them and specifically invited them to eat from. God said they could enjoy *all* but one (Gen. 2:16–17), yet Satan twisted things to look like God had said they couldn't have *any* of them. And by the time Satan had raised enough doubt in Eve's mind about why God didn't want them eating from the one forbidden tree, he'd tricked her into believing, despite the lavishness of the Lord's provision, that he was holding out on her. *If he really loved you,* Satan was saying, *if he really wanted the best for you—if he really wanted you wise and knowledgeable and able to reach your full potential—wouldn't he let you eat from this tree?*

Note Satan's method. He never told her a single thing. He *asked* her. It's so subtle, isn't it? Passive-aggressiveness at its finest. Or, you might say, its worst.

In that moment Eve made a choice. She chose to believe her enemy instead of her Creator. She chose to believe a lie about God's loving character and chose knowledge over love.

Not that we do that or anything.

After she ate it, she got Adam in on it too. Listen, Eve gets blamed a lot for this, but let's be honest: Adam still made the choice for himself.

I laugh when I read the part where God asked them what they'd done. (Incidentally, he already knew.) Adam pointed to Eve. Then Eve pointed to Satan. It's your classic "who gets the blame for ruining God's creation" game. It's also an example of how every human would act for the rest of time. We are awesome blame-shifters.

This moment is known as the Fall—an enormous little four-letter word that reframed the entire backdrop behind the story of Scripture. I'm not being overly dramatic in saying so. (Not that I *can't* be overly dramatic. I am fully capable. I blame it on my mom, who blames it on her mom, who blames it on Eve.) But the Fall truly changed every-thing, not only for Adam and Eve, but for all the rest of us going forward.

God, in his wisdom, had created the man and woman with the ability to choose whether or not to live in accor-dance with what he said was best for them. They opted out of that plan. They decided they wanted to have control more than love; knowledge more than relationship. They decided to trust themselves more than God and believed the lie that he was keeping something good away from them.

But their decision, the Bible says, shaped every person who would be descended from them, including us. Their disobedience resulted in separation from God, and it caused all the rest of us to be born in separation from him as well.

By Genesis 3 they'd already rebelled. As a result of their sin, death became a reality, and all of us are subject to it. The statistics are pretty strong; we aren't going to live (here) forever. Our human lives will end as a consequence of the sin that entered the world when Adam and Eve chose death over life.

Incidentally, a few days ago, one of the moms at the bus stop told us her daughter wanted to go play with her friends, and the mom told her she couldn't go, reminding her how we're currently in a pandemic and all. A few minutes later she overheard her daughter crying from her room, saying, "Why? Why did you eat the fruit, Eve???"

I've asked it a few times myself.

Not sure you believe that? Doesn't sound fair to you? You don't like how someone else's sin, way back when, should leave a permanent stain on us? As I said earlier, my deliberate purpose in journeying through this book with you is not to solve every *why;* it's to gain familiarity with *what* the Bible story and its message contains. And here's what it says:

> Sin came into the world through one man,
> and death through sin, and so death spread
> to all men because all sinned. (Rom. 5:12)

So that's where it started, and there's no going back now.

I promise this story is going to get better, but not for a little while yet, so just buckle up and stick with it.

Your and my sin—which, let's admit, we are thoroughly eaten up with—contains a source as old as Genesis 3 and comes with fruit as ripe and rotten as this morning. The root reason for why sin is *in* us is because our first parents decided not to trust God.

They fell.

And we became their fallen children.

HEART OF THE PROBLEM

All right, so we've got our first couple on earth, and they've ruined everything. Yay! I wouldn't really be so excited about this whole thing if I didn't know that God wasn't going to leave us this way. When you're the God of everything, you can find a workaround if you decide to. And the way he chose to do it is pretty unexpected. We'll get there.

So there was Creation, and then there was the Fall. I sure hope that fruit was good, because things were about to get real in Eden. As soon as they ate it, they realized something was off. They had never felt shame before. Up until then they'd been totally comfortable just cruising around in their birthday suits. I mean, it was only the two of them, so there weren't many curtains to close in the garden. But now it was different. Scripture says they heard God "walking in the garden in the cool of the day" (Gen. 3:8), and all they wanted was to get away from him.

I hardly ever got spanked when I was a kid because I was an angel (or a very good manipulator, with parents who hated to see me upset). But I'll tell you what. When I knew it was coming, the only thing I wanted to do was run as far away as I could and try to pad my pants so it wouldn't hurt as much.

I'm about to tell you a story that has never been printed before. I will warn you: it will forever change the way you think of me. This story is LEGENDARY in my family.

So there was this one time when I got in trouble because I wouldn't share my Etch-A-Sketch with my sister in the backseat, and my mom told me my dad was going to spank me as soon as he got home. I didn't believe her because I'd never been spanked before. Turns out I was wrong, and my sister had to leave my room, all the while staring at me in shock.

Dad decided I should have a bare-bottom spanking, and as he started to raise his hand, he noticed I was holding my breath and my face was turning bright red. He was concerned I wasn't breathing so he tried to comfort me.

And here's where it got real.

According to the legend (and I can tell you that I remember the T-shirt he was wearing because it is still so vivid in my mind), I turned my head and looked him in the eye, uttering words that would echo forever in my family: "I'm not holding my breath. I'm trying to poop on you so you will never do this to me again."

OKKKKAAAAYYYYYY, ANGELA.

Dad started laughing so hard that he had to leave the room.

And no, he never came back.

There's not really an amazing way to segue back to Adam and Eve hiding from God, so I'll give you a moment to compose yourself and then you can come right back.

Ready now? Here we go. God's first recorded words, found in Genesis 3:9 (and notice they're in the form of a question, as were the first recorded words of Satan):

"Where are you?"

Rest assured, he was not looking down into the garden, like, "Oh my gosh, these are my first people and I've already lost them. PERFECT." No, he knew where they were. He wasn't asking about their physical location; he was asking about the posture of their hearts toward him.

Satan asked them what they believed about God ("Did God actually say?"—*are you sure?*) and then God did the same ("Where are you?"). We answer these same questions every single day of our lives. How we answer them reflects which voice we're choosing to listen to.

I think for most people, the net result of interacting with God and with the teaching of his Word is guilt. Now I promise I'm fun, and—don't worry—we're going to *have* fun. But there's good reason for that guilt. Because we *are* guilty, like Adam and Eve were guilty. And a perfectly holy God deserves perfectly holy people, which is certainly not any one of us. With that said, I definitely dated a couple of people who would say they thought they were the exceptions. So much so that one of them cried when I broke up with him because he couldn't fathom how anyone wouldn't want to be with him. If you want to add to that visual, I am 5'1" and he was 6'7" and one of the best basketball players to come out of the city I'm from. He had a barbed wire tattoo on his bicep, and it somehow led to a slippery slope which included wearing sunglasses to parties when it was pitch-black dark outside. And to that, I say NO.

Where were we?

Ah, yes, the disillusion of perfection and the reality of our true condition.

But if that's where we think God wants to leave us—in our guilt—we're missing the point of who he is.

What we see in God's actions here is grace. Consequences? Sure. We'll look at those soon. But notice first of all—notice most of all—a God who was pursuing his people even after they'd sinned against him and failed to trust him. Their sin had provided ample evidence of the gap between their hearts and his holiness. I know this sounds pretty intense. And it is. But there's a difference between consequence and condemnation. Many people live in fear of the latter, imagining God as a dictator itching to turn on them for doing anything wrong. It's natural for us to feel that way. But that's not the point of this story. The beautiful part is that he didn't leave us there. He made a way instead.

So while Adam and Eve were cowering and trying to cover themselves with fig leaves (innovative, but unsuccessful), God made the first animal sacrifice in order to cover them up with loincloths. And this is what we in the business call "foreshadowing." Man, God is a really fantastic storyteller.

JESUS IN GENESIS

I want you to notice the order of God's responses to Adam and Eve's sin. Before he told them what their sin would inevitably cost them, he had a few uplifting words for the snake:

> "I will put enmity between you and the woman, and between your offspring and her offspring; he shall bruise your head, and you shall bruise his heel." (Gen. 3:15)

This might not actually sound all that exciting at this point, but here's what it's saying. Yes, Satan will "bruise the heel" of God's people. That's what you and I feel from him just about all the time, just about every day. Satan specializes in catering his bruises to us in the ways that most affect us—the things we can't stop disliking about ourselves, the regrets that never quite escape our thoughts.

He also knows another trick. He knows that even seemingly stupid things can get under our skin the most. You know, like not being able to find your keys or stubbing your toe. I would venture to say 90 percent of the arguments that Todd and I have had over the years (hypothetically) started out with something so absurd but then snowballed. We finally realized that somehow my tripping over his slipper led me down a path that ended up with me talking about a party where my first-grade teacher embarrassed me in front of the whole class because I ate only the frosting off two cupcakes. Obviously, to my mind, the path from the shoe to the cupcake was pure logic.

But, seriously, Satan loves throwing these "tiny" things my way, over and over. Because, I promise you, I'm your girl if you're ever in a crisis. I will hold it together and stay calm, rational, and empathetic. But if I can't remember the password for Netflix, I will lose my ever-loving mind and threaten to burn down the house. *Run from me.*

Well, tell me the password, and *then* run from me.

It leads me to tell you something that can often be hard to swallow, though we need to go ahead and put it in that "true mystery" category: *God has given our enemy permission to do this to us.* I know what you're thinking if all of this is new to you: "WHERE DO I SIGN UP?" But stick with me. Remember, there's an arc to the story.

A wound to the heel is only temporary, not lethal. Something can still be done to help you survive it and get over it. A crushing blow to the head though? That's how you *kill* a snake. All of its poison is located in the head—the head that will be crushed by the God who came to rescue us.

In other words, Satan's days are numbered.

So here's my version of what God was saying to Adam and Eve (and us): "The state you've placed yourself in is temporary. But out of my deep love for you, despite how little you deserve it, I will bring a solution to bridge the chasm between us."

Or to put it another way: the God who pursues us is not pursuing to punish us, but to provide us a plan for his loving redemption.

Prepare to see this heart of God on every page of the Bible. He is relentless in his pursuit of us, and the last thing we should feel is entitlement. We do terrible, hurtful, heartbreaking things that should push him away, and yet he takes the initiative to draw his people back into the circle of his protection and blessing. He responds to sin with forgiveness and restoration. He stands in the path of destruction and holds back the hopelessness that makes it feel so final.

Don't bother with the whole fig-leaves thing. He knows what you're trying to hide from him. What he wants from you is the same thing he wanted from Adam and Eve: to come to him, to cry out to him, to seek his mercy, and to stand on his truth and promises.

He loves us the same way he loved Adam and Eve: in spite of ourselves.

So before we move on, why don't you take a second to consider one of the most important questions that will ever be posed to you: What comes to mind when you think about God?

Chapter 3

LET'S TRY THIS AGAIN, SHALL WE?

The Flood and Its Aftermath

 Here's the part where Adam and Eve have been kicked out of the garden, and everyone is about to die. It's basically a Disney movie.

The thing is, when we're left to ourselves, we are going to find ways—to *seek* ways—to rebel against God, to subdue and overpower others, and try to work everything to our own advantage.

This is the mess we've fallen into, from Eden forward.

And the Bible is the story of God working to get us out of it.

As you can imagine, it's not a smooth ride.

Anyway, here we go: Genesis 4. The first two brothers. And already, the first murder conviction. Seriously. Adam and Eve's first son, Cain, killed their second son, Abel. Bless their poor mother's heart. The family beach picture didn't last long over the mantel.

But to understand this period of history, you need to know what was most important to these people. Simple: *having babies*. All the babies. So, for the next little bit of Scripture—up through Genesis 5 for now—the Bible takes us through a stretch of family lineage. Not many of the names are ones you'll remember or have heard too much about. I'll point out only a few of them.

There's Seth, for instance, the third son of Adam. Further down the list, Enoch is another name worthy of a mention. He "walked with God," the Bible says (Gen. 5:22), and amazingly never died. God just took him on up to heaven when it was his time to go, same as he did with the prophet Elijah hundreds of years later. Among the many sons of Enoch was Methuselah (I really dig his name and feel like it's underused), the oldest man who ever lived, all 969 years of him.

Let's be honest. If you're anything like me, you tend to glance over these long lists of typically unpronounceable names whenever they appear in Scripture, moving on to where the action starts again. But the truth is, these numbers that correspond to their life spans in Genesis 5 give us a clue about how much time passed after the events of the garden of Eden until the events of Genesis 6 took place.

Hundreds of years went by, and humanity was not on good behavior. Like, at all. They rejected anything God told them was good and made decisions that would top anyone's list of "please don't ever say that out loud again."

> The LORD saw that the wickedness of man was great in the earth, and that every intention of the thoughts of his heart was only evil continually. (Gen. 6:5)

Then comes this: "The LORD regretted that he had made man on the earth, and it grieved him to his heart" (v. 6). *Okay, but how do you really feel, God?* He knew the sin that was in their hearts, and he knew it would only get worse and pull them further away from him. So he did something subtle.

He killed everyone and called for a do-over.

There's a running joke with people who know me. I can't fix things midway and keep going. If I'm knitting, for example, and make a mistake, I'll give it about four minutes of trying to figure out how to patch it over, but if that doesn't work, I'll undo the whole thing. I just need a fresh start. If I'm going to rearrange a room, it needs to be totally empty before I start. It's the white paper with no marks. It's also why I have eighty-seven journals with only three entries in them.

So, I guess, in theory, I get this approach. But what kind of God wipes out all of humanity? Sounds like the kind of Father you would want, doesn't he? It's the kind of story that's made a lot of people question his goodness and his love. But we've got to back up a little and remember a few things:

1. *We're not God.* If this is news to you, I'm sorry, but I don't know how else to say it. We have no way to think the way God does or to imagine what we would do if we were in his place. All we need to remember is that he is good and he is *for* us. And I guess in this situation, he knew that the best way to start the redemption story over was to let the yarn unravel. Let's not think we know better. Let's not get too cocky in our own abilities and intelligence. We can barely parallel park.

2. *God is good, but he is also just.* Don't forget, there's this little matter of the people's every impulse, every thought of their hearts, being "only evil continually." What was God supposed to do with that? Give them a pep talk? Give them stickers? In what way would that have helped them? Also, there weren't any stickers yet, so that's a kink. They'd done nothing but wander away from him, to the point of daily despising him and ignoring every opportunity to humble themselves before him. They weren't just being decently moral and forgetting to do their quiet times. It wasn't like they were committing minor traffic violations and, bam, God wiped them out. No, they were being horrific—the kind of stuff you see on the news and gasp at, the kind of moral exceptions we make that tell us death wouldn't be a

severe enough punishment for, say, Adolph Hitler. In this point of human history, *everyone* was Hitler. Can you imagine? Every single person was as evil as humanly possible. I could list off a bunch of words that would make you get super uncomfortable, or make you want to go storm your local political office and demand change, like, right now, but I won't. Just imagine all those things in your head and then remember God said that humans were doing *only* these things. Not some good things too, mixed in with the bad. No. *Only* these bad things. All the time. Every day. Whether emotionally or physically, people were at their worst, harming themselves and harming others. That's not the kind of thing you can just paint over. They had to be dealt with. It's not like it was going to get better.

3. *God is love.* God is many things. He is entirely *separate* from us, meaning he doesn't think the way we think. He is entirely *sovereign*, meaning he has control over everything and can do whatever he wants, whenever he wants to do it. But above all, he is entirely loving. I'm not just trying to sound Christian-y by saying it. I don't have the bumper sticker. It's a true statement, and it's more than a catchy phrase. I hope you'll let it soak in as you head to the rest of the book:. "God is love" (1 John 4:8). And so we know his ultimate goal in what he did was somehow based on that love. He will never go against his nature or his promises.

Here's the thing. God is not our problem. *We* are our problem. *Our sin* is our problem. We are three-year-olds throwing a tantrum, and I think we all know how that shakes out.

Let me just say a quick something to you, if you know little to nothing of God or of Jesus. I don't blame you for wanting to close this book and move along to something happier, like a root canal, but it's going to get better. I'm not just trying to sound Christian-y by saying God is love.

I don't have the magnet, but I do know it's more than just a catchy phrase. I hope you'll let that sink in as you head to the rest of this book.

You may have had people in your life who pound the Bible over your head. (Anyone remember that crazy traveling preacher from *Little House on the Prairie*? Oh my gosh, and then when Mary screamed because she went blind? Or the freaky guy who came into town to sell his wares from some sort of traveling cart? I could go on.) But it still doesn't sound like a great PR campaign. We just need to understand we didn't get what we deserved. That's the best news ever. In fact, that's what the New Testament is all about—the good news. See? I told you there were brighter days ahead.

RAINED OUT, RAINED IN

R. C. Sproul, the late author and theologian (and one of my favorites), once looked back on his decades of teaching theology in the classroom and could think of countless examples when students had approached him with questions about why God doesn't just save *everybody*. Wouldn't that be truly merciful? Shouldn't that be the whole intent of his grace? Sproul said:

> Somewhere deep inside the secret chambers of our hearts, we harbor the notion that God owes us His mercy, that heaven would not be quite the same if we were excluded from it. We know we're sinners, but surely we're not as bad as we could be. There are enough redeeming features to our personalities that if God is really just, He will include us in salvation.[3]

Only once, he said, did a student come up to him and ask what all of us should actually be wondering: "Why did he redeem *me*?" And this next sentence—*gah*! I have to be honest. The first time I read it, I had to set my book down for a second because the words were so profound. "What amazes us is justice," Sproul concluded, "not grace." It's the difference between asking why God would ever cause a flood to wipe out the entire earth instead of asking him why he would let Noah and his family live.

We are amazed by justice because we expect grace. I deserved that spanking, but I didn't get it. And that's where the analogy ends because I think we all know the next part does not apply in this context.

Okay, time to meet Noah—you know, the one who walked onto a boat with animals going two by two? Anyway, he's about to walk into his starring role right here, and listen—he's a good guy.

The Lord told Noah that he was going to send a great flood, and Noah's job was to build an ark that God would use to save him and his family, not to mention a bunch of random animals. You may have figured out why they were going two by two. They'd eventually be tasked with repopulating the world, so it made sense for their job to be reproductively possible.

God gave Noah specific instructions for the dimensions, the materials, and the construction process for the ark, and he apparently got right to work—though, as you can imagine, he became the town's biggest source of gossip. He was literally hammering together pieces of wood and building a boat for a flood that God had told him was going to come. It was like . . .

> NOAH: Good news, folks! This boat is going
> to save my family and me!

PEOPLE: *What?!* (What *is* it with this guy?)

NOAH: Bad news, folks . . . (look of realization, solemn silence, before turning slowly and walking back to his pile of wood)

After a long time, though, the big day finally came. Noah closed up the ark, along with the pairs of animals on board, even the ones that were considered "not clean" (Gen. 7:2), which we'll learn more about in Leviticus 11. I'm sure you're on the edge of your seat with anticipation about that. I can feel it. With all the other animals—the "clean" ones (v. 2)—God told Noah to round up and bring aboard *seven* pairs each. And there's a majorly significant reason for that, which I'll explain in just a minute.

So it rained. A lot. For forty days and forty nights. I've been on road trips with my family that lasted all of seven hours but felt like an eternity. Let's just say I really wouldn't want to be stuck on a boat with my sweaty, dirty family and pigeon poop. Incidentally, the number *forty* almost always indicates a season of personal testing. We're going to see it in a bunch of other places, so just keep it in the back of your mind for now.

Finally the 40 days ended. And they jumped off the boat and lived their best lives. *Untrue.* It was just the dysfunctional party that kept on giving. They had to wait another 150 days for the water to recede. Do you know what the number 150 means in the Bible? Actually, I don't think it means anything, except QUALITY FAMILY TIME ON THE LIDO DECK. And even after that, when it came time to disembark, imagine the stark reality of discovering that all the family therapists had been wiped off the face of the earth too. This was less than optimal, because it had been a hard season and all.

Guess what Noah did as soon as he got off the ark? He built an altar to the Lord, then he selected some of the clean animals and offered them as burnt offerings. These clean animals were not only the ones that were considered most fitting for food; they were also the most fitting for an offering to God as a symbol of worship. That's why they needed seven pairs of these, to help the repopulation scheme go a little more quickly.

Speaking of repopulation, I'm just going to set this down and you can pick it up at your leisure. It was just Noah and his family on the boat, so they were the only ones who were alive to do the job. *"I'll take 'Awkward Gender Reveal Parties' for $400, Alex."*

So here we have the first time a person sacrificed animals to seek atonement for sins. All this means is that we have a need to reconcile ourselves to God, to fill the gap in our relationship with him. And during this time period, it was done through animal sacrifice.

Couple of thoughts on that:

1. *Animal sacrifices were modeled by God and required by him.* If you'll remember, soon after God's pronouncement of sin's curse following Adam and Eve's fall in the garden, God made clothes for Adam and Eve from animal skins. Atonement was made, but it came at the cost of a life. An animal must be slain.

2. *Sacrifice was pleasing and acceptable to God.* He deemed Noah's offering to be honorable and good. God's solution to mankind's sin came with a debt. Remember, atonement via sacrifice is a payment. As with any wrongdoing, somebody has to pay. And so for Noah, through sacrifice, restored relationship with God could become reality. Keep this in mind as we go. Because, trust me, it'll hit you really hard later on when we move into the New Testament.

Let me interject here: I don't like the whole animal sacrifice thing at all, and to be honest I struggled with understanding how a loving God would allow such a brutal thing to happen. I probably would've tried to save all of them because there's a zero percent chance that I could stomach a sacrifice. I wish it hadn't been that way, and I can't tell you I can explain it perfectly, so I'll just say it's okay if it bothers you, but we've got to trust that God is good and that we aren't him.

This flood also came with a promise, a covenant that God was making with his people. We'll be talking about covenant a lot more in the next chapter when we get to Abraham, but we've already seen a couple of them. Remember when God told Adam that if he ate from the forbidden tree he would "surely die" (Gen. 2:17)? This was basically the first covenant in the Bible, saying that if mankind would obey God perfectly, none of us would ever know death. (THANKS A LOT, EVE, AND CAN WE HAVE A SIT-DOWN WHEN I MEET YOU?) But then God promised to crush Satan's head (Gen. 3:15), remember? That was a covenant, too, that God would do something himself to rescue us from our sin. And now, after this cruise on the ark, God instituted another covenant. He painted a rainbow in the sky and gave his word that there would never be another flood.

> "I have set my bow in the cloud, and it shall be a sign of the covenant between me and the earth. When I bring clouds over the earth and the bow is seen in the clouds, I will remember my covenant that is between me and you and every living creature of all flesh. And the waters shall never again become a flood to destroy all flesh." (Gen. 9:13–15)

And when God makes a covenant, he keeps it.

So here's the takeaway, friend. Evil people doing evil things was terrible, and the flood that God sent to stop it all was terrible. But the new start came with the promise of God that this was the last time he would do such things to humanity. That's good news, yes? With sin's curse all around us and inside us, God has chosen by his grace to give us another chance.

I've never been so grateful for shuffleboard and buffets in my life.

THROUGH GENESIS AND BEYOND

Genesis 10 kicks off with a partial list of my ex-boyfriends. (College was a BUSY SEASON.) Actually, it's the lineage of Noah's three kids: Shem, Ham, and Japheth. And they did not mess around with God's commandment to "be fruitful and multiply." Here's where we see the population start to grow larger and larger as the many generations come and go.

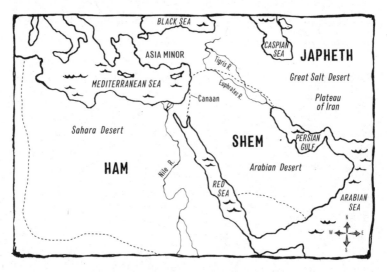

NOAH'S SONS: WHERE THEY WENT

I've included a little map for you on the previous page so you can see what I'm talking about. Notice how each of the sons of Noah and their descendants gravitated into three separate regions. They were like, "I will look back on the boat season with as much fondness as I can muster, but I think it's time we put some healthy space between us. Let's plan on holidays at Shem's and birthdays at Ham's."

Japheth's people moved north and northwest, up into what became known as Asia Minor (basically, modern-day Turkey), as well as the islands of the Mediterranean, like Cyprus and Crete, even as far west as the later nations of Greece and Italy. I love how beautiful this all looks on paper. I can barely get to the grocery store without getting lost, and I just used the phrase "modern-day Turkey" in a sentence.

Ham and his offspring drifted south and southwest, into North Africa, toward the territories that would become Egypt and the Sudan. They also occupied the land of Canaan, and would turn out to be the folks that we'll see the Israelites encounter later in the story when they get to the Promised Land. (Best story ever. Almost.) These people were not gentle or kind. They were rowdy troublemakers. They went by names like the Amorites and Jebusites and Perizzites and lots of other "ites." Don't get too bogged down with the names. They aren't on the test.

Then there's *Shem* and the generations that descended from his family. They flowed eastward into the Arabian peninsula, which is where Abraham would eventually come from. We keep talking about Abraham like he's going to be some kind of big deal in the Bible. Listen—you have no idea. You're going to love him. Also, I want you to start picking up on the fact that the Bible actually connects to the world we live in today, because many of the things you hear on the news or in conversation will sound different when you start to make these connections. For example, you can hear the faint shadow of Shem's name in the ethnic word *Semites* or *Semitic,* probably most often heard in its negative form—*anti-Semitic*—referring to those who are racially biased against Jews. Yet another reminder to us all that, yes, *the Bible really happened.*

That's where the crew ended up. Even if it looks foreign to you now, we'll come back to it in later chapters, so I wanted you to have a visual. That's also why, instead of sticking the maps way in the back, where they usually go, I've brought them right up here into the heart of the action. I feel sorry for maps, you know? When it comes to the world of emojis, they're the stock market graph. They desperately want to be the crying happy face, or even the red heart or the flamenco dancer, but alas, their fate is to be six swipes away.

We take this moment to honor you, maps. Welcome to the first screen. This is your fifteen minutes.

JOB: A GENESIS INTERLUDE

Remember when I told you the Bible wasn't necessarily in order? Okay, so here's our first example of that. The eighteenth book of the Bible is named Job (pronounced "Jobe," remember), but it doesn't happen after the first seventeen books have passed. It likely happened around the same time of Genesis, though it doesn't show up there.

Hey, I didn't write the Bible. I'm just trying to make sense of it. Trust me, this next part is important, and I promise you can understand it and tuck it into your Rolodex of Bible knowledge.

The first five books of Scripture—Genesis through Deuteronomy—are the books of law. The Jews call them the *Torah*, which is the Hebrew word for "law." They're also known as the Pentateuch, meaning "five books." They cover God's dealings with his people from the beginning of time to their possession of Canaan, the Promised Land.

(If these events don't mean anything to you yet, that's fine. We'll get to all that.)

Next are twelve books of history—Joshua through Esther—which travel in more or less a straight line chronologically, picking up where Deuteronomy leaves off.

Then comes Job. The book that bears his name doesn't include any references to other historical events, so there's not much to pull from in trying to time-stamp it. But based on the usage of language and other embedded clues that people a lot smarter than me can discern and speak knowledgeably about, it's quite possible Job lived sometime shortly after the flood. Maybe not, but likely so. I wasn't there, so the multiple-choice question would be a matter of odds. I'm not losing sleep over it. There are going to be a ton of times in this book where we just have to say, "You know what? I don't get it. But I don't want the details to hide the main story because that's the thing that ultimately matters the most."

These are people writing about events they remembered and describing what they'd seen and heard, as well as what information had been passed down throughout the generations. Honestly, I think the beauty of the way the Bible is written is that it allows room for humanity and divinity to collide. It is inspired by the Holy Spirit and written by average people doing their best to record facts.

I think the book of Job is one of the most difficult in the Bible to understand, teach, and embrace. Still, we're to believe the things we learn from it, even where we can't explain it.

It's written about a man who suffered immensely. He lost his family, his health, and his vast property holdings in a shockingly short amount of time. Through a remarkable piece of biblical revelation, the opening chapters pull back a curtain on the wider spiritual world, showing God giving Satan permission to inflict damage on Job's life, his children, his body, and his many possessions. God, in fact, is the one who pointed out Job as an example of the kind of person most likely to get under Satan's skin: "There is none like him on the earth, a blameless and upright man, who fears God and turns away from evil" (Job 1:8).

Yeah. That'll give you some deep thoughts.

Satan wanted to play ball, so he accused God of choosing Job for this experiment because of how easy a life the guy had. *He's got it so good, why WOULDN'T he trust you?* Then Satan upped the ante. He dared God to allow everything to be taken from Job—*then we'll see if he still calls you good and faithful:* "Stretch out your hand and touch all that he has, and he will curse you to your face" (v. 11).

For reasons we won't understand on this side of heaven, God agreed. And Satan began stripping Job's life away, one painful piece at a time, until the weight of the accumulated losses had nearly killed him.

Why would God allow such a thing? What kind of loving God would willingly let one of his loved ones be treated this way?

I hear you, friend. And I've asked the same things myself. The severity of Job's challenges feels cruel and unnecessary as we turn those pages. But all I know to say is this, something I've already said before: I believe God is good, even when I don't understand what he's doing.

And trust me, I do not say these words flippantly. I say them as a woman who's stood in a cemetery on a warm April day and watched my daughter being lowered into the ground. And with the thud of each shovelful of dirt that physically separated me from her, I was forced to make a decision about the God who allowed it.

Either he loves me or he doesn't.
Either he is good or he is not.

And in time, I landed on what I believe. Not based on emotion. Not based on shallow hope. Frankly, I chose the only place that proved safe enough for me to rest my weary bones in it.

I believe God does love me.
I believe God is good.

And I believe Job chose the same thing. Otherwise, he wouldn't have been able to say through his pain, "I know that my Redeemer lives, and at the last he will stand upon the earth. And after my skin has been thus destroyed, yet in my flesh I shall see God" (Job 19:25–26).

He stayed faithful through it all.

This does not, however, mean that he never grieved or questioned. Faithfulness is not the ability to push our feelings and doubts aside and pretend we're totally okay with whatever is happening.

I was twenty weeks pregnant when I found out my daughter Audrey couldn't live outside of my body, and I chose to carry her as long as I could in the hopes of a miracle.

She lived for two and a half hours, just long enough to change all of us.

So was I faithful? I believe I was. I mean, I tried to be.

But let me also tell you that I went to a baby shower a few days after my diagnosis and hugged the guest of honor while our stomachs touched. Everyone there was trying to figure out how to let sorrow and joy dance together, and we all just did the best we could.

On the way home, I screamed at God.

Screamed.

Until my throat felt scratchy and my eyes were dripping mascara onto my face.

I was furious. I was devastated. I was so confused that I couldn't make sense of anything, let alone the God who knew that a doctor was about to walk into my exam room and tell me I would never braid my daughter's hair.

If anyone ever tells you that you can't question God or be angry with him, they don't know the many passages in Scripture that disagree. We can't love God the way he wants us to love him if we remain in a pit of doubt and anger, but this doesn't mean we have to shut off our humanity in order to be faithful.

Bring it all to him, friend.

I assure you of two things: he already knows how you feel, and he wants you to bring it to him. He isn't intimidated by your questions and isn't angered by your doubt. He loves you. And in a little while, we're going to learn the degree to which he was willing to go to in order to truly understand how it feels to live in flesh while wrestling in a broken world.

FROM BABEL ON

So here's something shocking: people love feeling a sense of power, and they often overestimate their own importance. The consistent nature of human beings is to exalt themselves and their names above God and his name.

It's a theme we won't see disappearing anytime soon in our travels along the story line of Scripture. You would think that after God wiped out the entire world, the new folks would want to tiptoe around anything that might get them in trouble with a God powerful enough to cause a flood, but humility didn't last too long.

> "Come, let us build ourselves a city and a tower with its top in the heavens, and let us make a name for ourselves, lest we be dispersed over the face of the whole earth." (Gen. 11:4)

Well, that sounds like a plan that honors God, right? "Round up everyone, because we're going to build a little something and then become great." God isn't unclear about how these things tend to go. "Those who walk in pride he is able to humble" (Dan. 7:34). So God decided he would take away one of the main building blocks that supported their expansion project, and that was the end of that.

Up until then, all humanity spoke a common language, which contributed to their ability to join together as one body in conspiring and constructing their own little kingdom. But in referring to those who rallied around this building campaign, God said, "let us go down and there confuse their language, so that they may not understand one another's speech" (Gen. 11:7). Suddenly, people who'd been in such like-minded agreement couldn't get along with each other, and their dreams of a tower that they could name after themselves received a name more befitting the pointlessness of their project.

> Therefore its name was called Babel, because there the LORD confused the language of all the earth. And from there the LORD dispersed them over the face of all the earth. (v. 9)

Womp, womp. You didn't get your tower. You wanted to get higher and closer to being God, and he reminded you that your futile efforts will always end up this way. Even Satan himself is a fallen angel. He once existed alongside God, but he couldn't stand to be inferior to him, so he tried to raise himself up to a level he could never reach. But he fell, and now he roams the earth in battle against the One he couldn't overcome. And can't overcome. And will never overcome.

But I'm getting ahead of myself. Let's go ahead and meet this Abraham fellow we've been referring to. Trust me, his story will not disappoint. Spoiler alert: people lived a looooooong time back then, and somehow they still found a way to, umm, populate the earth while stocking up on Metamucil and shower seats.

So, the therapists are back, the babies are keeping the midwives busy, and there are no towers that reach heaven. All is well until it's not.

Chapter 4

THIS OLD (FAMILY) MAN
Covenant with Abraham

I know you've been holding your breath and waiting for Terah, and I'm so glad you can finally exhale. Terah was a great-great-great-great-great-great-grandson of Shem. Remember him? He and his brother Japheth were the kind of guys everyone wants in their fraternity. Their dad Noah gave them the blessing that was supposed to go to their older brother Ham because they were kind enough to cover him up when they found him drunk and naked in his tent (see Gen. 9:23). I have no details about what led to their finding him in that predicament, but I will tell you I was often the hair holder for friends who needed a Shem.

Seven generations later, Terah was born into Shem's family line.

Now for reasons which the Bible doesn't tell us, except that one of his sons had died before him, Terah decided to pick up and leave home and head off to a distant land, toward Canaan. Check out the map I've inserted for you on the next page that traces the path of their journey. In terms of modern-day geography, the itinerary had them leaving the region we now know as Iraq, heading northwest, then taking a southerly route down into Canaan, where Israel is located today, surrounded by its Arab neighbors. Terah left with his grown son Abram (yeah, his name was just Abram at first), along with Abram's wife, Sarai, and also with his

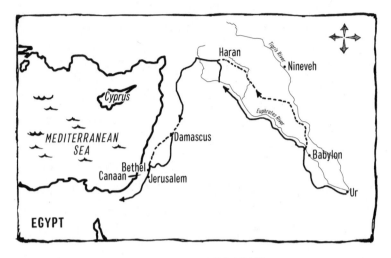

ABRAHAM LEAVES HOME

nephew Lot, the one whose father (Terah's son Haran) had passed away. (I know, it's a lot of names, but try to stay tuned because you'll get the hang of it and you'll be so proud of yourself.)

So, more happy news: Terah bit the dust before they made it to Canaan.

Now we're ready to jump into one of the most important stories in the entire Bible. And who saw it coming in only the twelfth chapter of Genesis? That was rhetorical. Seriously, if you miss what happens here, you honestly won't be able to understand the whole rest of Scripture as a story. It'll just seem like a series of disjointed episodes held together by the common thread of, "and here's where another person with a ridiculous name dropped dead." I'm saying a lot, I realize, but it's true. Because here, in this short account of God's words to Abram, he inserted a critical stitch into the story of his loving plans for a chosen group of people:

Now the LORD said to Abram, "Go from your country and your kindred and your father's house to the land that I will show you. And I will make of you a great nation, and I will bless you and make your name great, so that you will be a blessing. I will bless those who bless you, and him who dishonors you I will curse, and in you all the families of the earth shall be blessed." (Gen. 12:1–3)

Time now to put some meaning behind these words.

- Where did the Lord want Abram to go?
- And what did he tell him would happen?

Do you already know all this? Not really? Maybe vaguely familiar? Do you have all the answers memorized in Hebrew, Greek, French, and Italian? Good for you. Now please leave. You are not my target audience. I'm secretly hoping it didn't make any sense at all to you, and that you're dying to see how the puzzle pieces start moving into place to make these things happen.

Specifically, where did God tell Abram to go? Do you see anything that clearly says? In those verses? Yeahhhhhhh . . . he didn't exactly add that part to the itinerary. God told Abram to leave everything behind and keep heading in the general direction of a "land that I will show you." That's all the clarification he was going to get. But, to the second question ("What did he tell him would happen?"), God gave Abram the silver lining of future *greatness* as an added incentive—the prospect of a great nation, the promise of a great name. Still, it was a big ask to make of a man fairly new at being a nomad. Wouldn't it at least have been nice to have a quick clarifying convo regarding travel plans?

Maybe a couple of Hilton reservations on the way? That's tricky, though, because most of them don't take camels.

We see this happen over and over again in Scripture. God will tell a person to go somewhere or do something without giving them all the details, requiring them to trust him implicitly, despite how unlikely the outcome seems. When he did it with Abram, what happened next? Three words from Genesis 12:4 summarize the life of a man who would change history forever.

So Abram went.

I'm pretty sure I would have done the same. I love the thought of gathering up my life and dragging my kids across a hot desert that has no end in sight. SOMEONE PUT SUNSCREEN ON TERAHBRAZITE.

When they finally got to Canaan, the Lord appeared to Abram again, telling him that he and his family could go ahead and set up camp there because this was where God wanted them. This was the land he was giving both to him and his descendants. So break out the pots and pans, Sarai. Time to bake up some fun things to take to your neighbors. (And also, Sarai, it's not going to go well for you here. Don't say I didn't warn you.)

What did loyal Abram do when God said this was the place? He found a hair holder and went for it. No, not at all. This guy is the real deal. He built an altar there. He was definitely Teacher's pet.

I just had a random memory pop into my head as I wrote that. When I was in college, we had a teacher who told us he altered our grades based on where we chose to sit in class. He called the back row "slack-jawed mouth-breathers." Wasn't much "teacher's pet" material back there.

Wait, where were we?

What we're witnessing here is another *covenant*. Another huge, huge covenant. It is so huge, in fact, that

God wasn't quite finished revealing the whole thing to him. It was a lot for one sitting.

We'll pick up the story now in Genesis 13, where we learn that Lot and Abram had too many livestock for the land to handle, so they decided to split up. (Lot was Abram's nephew and a serious troublemaker who wasn't super concerned about the consequences of his actions.) Abram, in a classy act of humility and wisdom, told Lot to pick the land he wanted first: "If you take the left hand, then I will go to the right, or if you take the right hand, then I will go to the left" (v. 9). He was such a giver, that Abram.

Foolish Lot preferred the looks of a valley down near the Dead Sea which seemed particularly lush and fertile, "well watered everywhere like the garden of the LORD" (v. 10). But to put it into perspective, there were a couple of cities down there named Sodom and Gomorrah. We'll get there, but just know that these folks make Noah's rager look like a third-grade birthday party.

Also, Lot? I don't have time to tell your story here, but I'm sorry your wife was disobedient and turned into a pillar of salt.

Abram, however, ended up in the pasturelands of Canaan, where God took him aside again for some Q.T. and said this:

> "Lift up your eyes and look from the place
> where you are, northward and southward
> and eastward and westward, for all the land
> that you see I will give to you and to your
> offspring forever." (Gen. 13:14–15)

And that's not all: "I will make your offspring as the dust of the earth" (v. 16), as uncountable as the grains of sand beneath all the acreage around him as far as Abram could see. In fact, God invited him to take a little tour, to "walk through the length and the breadth of the land" (v. 17) and feast his eyes on everything he was preparing to give him.

Abram was a man of integrity. His desire was to honor what the Lord was asking of him. It's just that, unfortunately, there was a teensy-weensy, itty-bitty detail that hadn't been addressed yet. "God? Heyyyyyyy . . . you know I'm the kind of guy who wants to be obedient to you, but as it turns out, I have no kids and my wife is barren. We've been AARP members for eight decades." (That's Genesis 15:2–3, as modified by yours truly.) Abram loved the idea of all his heirs getting the land. Except that there *weren't* any. And he and Sarai were already late for their Silver Sneakers class at the Y.

So Abram gently brought up the topic. But God was unwavering. *You WILL have a child. YOU. And SARAI.* I'm sure Abram just kind of nodded and started working through how he was going to break the news to his wife. God bless the woman, she probably just wanted to sleep. And yet she was about to be part of one of the most significant moments of all time. So she was going to need a cup of coffee, and (as I mentioned) a hair holder, because morning sickness is surely worse when you're ten thousand years old. (That's not the actual number, but when it comes to childbirth, it might as well be.)

God wasn't done. He had told Abram his heirs would be greater than the number of grains of sand that exist. And now, under a speckled sky, he offered another image:

> "Look toward heaven, and number the stars,
> if you are able to number them." Then he
> said to him, "So shall your offspring be."
> (v. 5)

To prove it, the Lord invited Abram to a ritual. A *covenant* ritual.

Oftentimes in those days, when two people entered into a covenant together, the two parties would divide a sacrifice. Translation: they would kill some animals, cut them in half, then walk a figure-eight pattern between them while reciting the conditions of their deal. The only thing I associate with a figure eight is my parents telling me not to talk to the fifty-something-year-old guy who did them in the middle of the roller-skating rink every Saturday.

But this deal was different, thank goodness. Implied in the gruesome demonstration was the idea that if one of the agreeing parties failed to uphold their end of bargain, um . . . let's just say the result wouldn't be pretty for that person. (Yes, you are guessing correctly. If someone failed to do their part of the bargain, they were basically saying, "may what has happened to these animals happen to me." *That's* how strong someone's word was, back in the day. If you promised, you followed through!) But this time, with all the animals gutted into position—a heifer, a goat, a ram, along with a dove and a young pigeon—God did something a little different. Verse 12 says a "deep sleep" fell over Abram. God didn't even want him *awake* for this process. I wonder if that option would be available to Sarai later when she went into labor. I mean, she must have been rickety.

Why didn't God want Abram to be awake for this?

Because it wasn't a mutual agreement.

God wasn't obligating Abram to do anything in order to make and uphold this covenant. God was taking full responsibility for keeping the covenant himself. His promise would stand no matter what. The reason Abram didn't need to be awake for it—the reason he didn't need to play any kind of active role in its inception—was because God's commitment to Abram was the only thing that mattered.

> He [Abram] believed the LORD, and he [God]
> counted it to him as righteousness. (Gen.
> 15:6)

God would do the walking around and the promising and the covenant making. Abe would just, you know, lie there asleep. So what God was saying, in essence, is this: "Abram, I'll do my part *and* I'll do your part. If I don't do my part, may what's been done to the animals be done to me. And if you do don't do *your* part, may what's been done to the animals *be done to me, too.* If you mess up, I'll pay for it." God was taking responsibility for both halves of the equation. He was going to pull off this whole thing, all the way through.

In short, God would do the doing; all Abram needed to do was believe.

Sound like the New Testament gospel to you? *Just believe,* God says. That's the requirement. *The rest is on me,* he says, and he will never break his word.

So here's where we get an early glimpse of the wild mercy of God.

He wanted the best for them.

He wants the best for us.

The words of this covenant are still impacting us, which makes this a moment for you to think about a fact you may not have considered . . .

> Not only is the Bible one story,
> it's a story you are now a part of.

"In you all the families of the earth shall be blessed" (Gen. 12:3). A covenant. A gospel covenant.

Dear Abram.

Sweet Sarai.

Listen, you two. Things are going to get a little upside-down for a bit. But out of all the things you don't know yet, here's the best part: out of all the stars in the sky, there is one that shines the brightest. We aren't going to meet him for a little while, but know this: he will be born in an obscure town in the most unlikely way possible. And just like God promised, when our part of the covenant is broken, he will be the One to pay.

As Abram stared at the sky, he couldn't have possibly known what we know now: from his own lineage, one single star would come to save the world.

WHILE YOU WAIT

Well, he couldn't have known. By the time he came back to his senses, Abram was just focused on his next task.

Baby-making.

I need you to know I am a God-loving woman who is also as sarcastic as the day is long, and you have no idea how much I am holding my tongue right now. I wonder if Abram waited until Sarai's evening meds to break the news. *Perfect, Abe, we just got here, and we're about to be the freaks of Canaan.* But here's the thing. Remember when God didn't tell them exactly where they were going? Well, he did it again here. He didn't mention exactly how long it would be until this miracle baby would be born. Abram was fine with that (biting my tongue again), but Sarai was not as invested in the plan after several years passed. Because, tired.

So she came up with a clever new plan. And by "clever," I mean "huge mistake."

Hey, Abram! [Yes, dear.] *You know my maidservant Hagar?* [Yes, dear.] *I think you should marry her and have a baby with her, because then that baby would be considered mine.*

Abram surely froze and wondered if this was one of those, "Hey, Abey Baby, do I look 120,000 years old to you?"

moments. But he was a champ, so he decided to take one for the team. How sweet.

I'll skip some details here, but long story short (because date night really takes a hit in this kind of arrangement), Hagar conceived Abram's child. This caught Sarai in the oh-so-common place where she was feeling all of her feelings and suddenly wasn't super happy about Hagar's baby bump or the way her servant was now acting superior to her elders.

Sensing trouble, Hagar ran away and ended up in the desert, where God stopped her and told her to go back to Sarai's house and just deal with it, because there was something she didn't know about this baby she was carrying. This was such a tender moment between her and God. In the midst of that sacred silence, he told her that her baby would be the father of a significant race. (*Starts to turn around.) Also, according to Genesis 16:12, he was going to be a "wild donkey of a man." (*Record scratch, but also a solid baby shower theme, AM I RIGHT?)

Abram was eighty-six years old when his sweet lil' donkey boy was born.

A dozen years of awkward family photos passed, and everyone assumed this precious son was the promised child. His name was Ishmael, which is a name you'll want to hang on to as we go. My math skills are subpar, but these years put Abram reallllllllyyyy close to the three-digit age zone, when God came around again with an update:

> "No longer shall your name be called Abram, but your name shall be Abraham, for I have made you the father of a multitude of nations." (Gen. 17:5)

There are only a few times in the Bible when God changed someone's name. I'm just spitballing here, but it seems like there had already been a plethora of other opportunities. Exhibit A: HAM.

And yet this was the first. God changed Abram's name to *Abraham*—from "noble father" to "father of nations"—and changed Sarai's name to *Sarah*, a variation on the word "princess," enlarging it to mean "a princess to many." But why? It's because this covenant he was making with them would change not only human history but also the human heart. And it would start by changing *these* two people: Abraham and Sarah. Their change of name signified that God, by keeping his promise to them, was making them entirely new people, the people he'd always known they would become.

Also, Abraham? As a way of welcoming you to your new name and new life . . .

Time to get circumcised!

Does anyone else hear the faint sound of Sarah laughing?

At the age of ninety-nine, Abraham—as well as every male member of his family—went under the knife. PARTY AT ABRAHAM'S, Y'ALL!!!!! WHO'S BRINGING CHIPS?

Again, why? It does feel like an odd plot twist. But here's what you need to know for later when we get to the New Testament. The idea of *flesh* is often used in Scripture as a synonym for human sinfulness. And so this procedure of cutting flesh away, as was done here in circumcision, became a symbol of what this covenant was designed to accomplish in our hearts.

Eventually we're going to hang out with a guy named Paul, one of my favorite people in the Bible, and you will see a connection you may never have seen between this Old Testament covenant and the New Testament covenant.

Maybe Canaan isn't as far away from you as you think it is.

COVENANT CHILD

Soon thereafter, three men arrived at Sarah and Abraham's home. Two of them, we learn later, were actually angels. The third was the Lord himself, which is an incredibly rare occurrence known as a *theophany*. Not that you didn't know that. We'll come across a few more of these in the Bible, but just note that Abraham was one of the few people who got to have this experience where God actually appeared to him. When he did, the Lord encouraged Abraham to believe in the promise he had given him, and told him that he would have a baby (with Sarah) within the year.

Turns out, Sarah was listening as this conversation went down, and she couldn't hold back her laughter. The best part is that God told her she shouldn't have been laughing about it, and she told him she hadn't been. He was all, *Yeah, you did. I'm God, and I heard you.*

Read the room, Sarah.

Sure enough, they did have that son, and they named him Isaac. Remember when God told Abraham that the promised child would come through him and his wife? Yeah, he meant that.

And so, with Isaac here now, Sarah decided that Hagar and her son Ishmael were basically no longer necessary. One day she overheard Ishmael teasing Isaac at a party (Isaac was a toddler at the time) and she lost it. Last straw. She told Abraham to send them away.

But remember the prophecy that God gave to Hagar when she was pregnant? The part about her "wild donkey" becoming the father of a massive nation? Well, it turns out he did. You and I know them today as the *Arabs*. His brother Isaac, on the other hand, became the father of the *Jews*. They despised each other then, and they despise each other now. And still today, wherever you get your news from, you're constantly reminded this wasn't a story that faded away centuries ago.

Whenever I'm reading my Bible and I start to see a connection like this, a little voice in the back of my head whispers, "Wait, so this stuff is REAL?" *Yes*—yes, it is. The anger and hatred in the Middle East that is boiling over right this minute, at this very hour, originated with this one father and these two mothers who lived several thousand years ago.

We're going to skip over to Genesis 22 to pick up where this left off.

For those keeping score, we're now four chapters into this book I've written, this book you're reading about the entire Bible, and we haven't gotten through Genesis yet.

But that's okay. Because hidden there in the text of these chapters, written in a time period we might consider irrelevant to the present day, Jesus was whispering to us.

Isaac may have been the promised child, but he won't be the last.

AMAZING GRACE

Things were quiet for a little while, following the forced removal of Hagar and Ishmael. But the next time we hear Isaac's name in the Bible, it comes inside a doozy of a story. Out of the blue, God said to Abraham:

> "Take your son, your only son Isaac, whom you love, and go to the land of Moriah, and offer him there as a burnt offering on one of the mountains of which I shall tell you."
> (Gen. 22:2)

And what did Abraham do?

> He cut the wood for the burnt offering and
> arose and went to the place of which God
> had told him. (v. 3)

In other words, *"So Abraham went."*

Now listen again to the gist of what God was saying: "You know the son I promised you, Abraham? The one I said would one day father many nations? The one you love? *Him?* I need you to go out and start walking. *With him.* I'll show you along the way exactly where to go. Oh, and when you get there, you need to set him on an altar and kill him. GODSPEED AND GOOD LUCK."

Giddy-up, Isaac, we're going on an adventure.

In all seriousness, this situation brings up a topic that is often confusing: the difference between "tempting" and "testing."

God *tested* Abraham—and tests us—by putting us into situations where we're set up to honor him. When we exercise our faith in him amid the test, we discover how he gives us the ability to make choices that reflect our trust and love for him. Through his power at work in us, he gives us the opportunity to succeed, which is what he wants for us in the first place. *Testing* makes us better.

Tempting someone is the opposite of that. Tempting someone puts them in a situation where you want them to fail. If I happen to know you're dieting, and I wave a candy bar in front of your face, that's tempting. I'm deliberately trying to make you crack—which is how *Satan* works, not God. We can never blame our temptations on God.

Abraham passed the test. After hearing God speak, "Abraham rose early in the morning, saddled his donkey, and took two of his young men with him, and his son Isaac" (Gen. 22:3). He was obedient to a situation that made absolutely no sense to him because he trusted God more than what he could see with his own eyes.

Here we are then, with Abraham on the mountain. God had shown him the exact place where he was to slaughter Isaac—"your only son Isaac, whom you love."

Want to hear something really cool? This is the first time the word *love* is mentioned in the Bible, and it is referring to the love a father has for his only son. So beautiful.

So Abraham built the altar. He tied up his son. He laid him on top of it and held a knife above him. I can't help but wonder what Isaac was thinking right then. I mean, he'd gone there in agreement with his father. He hadn't tried to stop him. If this doesn't scream, FOLLOW UP WITH SOME ROLE-PLAYING THERAPY, I don't know what does.

> The angel of the LORD called to him from heaven and said, "Abraham, Abraham! . . . Do not lay your hand on the boy or do anything to him, for now I know that you fear God, seeing that you have not withheld your son, your only son, from me." (vv. 11–12)

Then Abraham "lifted up his eyes and looked . . ." Again, his every move was dictated by the Lord's commands.

> And behold, behind him was a ram, caught in a thicket by his horns. And Abraham went and took the ram and offered it up as a burnt offering instead of his son. (v. 13)

I want you to notice something that I didn't notice myself for a long time. When Isaac had asked along the way, *Hey, aren't we missing something, Dad?*—Abraham said not to worry, that God would provide a "lamb" for the sacrifice (v. 8). But what did Abraham actually see and then sacrifice?

A ram.

So where was the lamb? The lamb that would take the place of the person who was supposed to be sacrificed? Wait for it . . .

Two thousand years later, not too far away from this very place, the Lamb of God would be there, where he would sacrifice himself to save the sons and daughters he loves. He would carry the wood of his sacrifice on his back as he walked to his death. And he would do it in agreement with his Father.

I know, I know. I'm getting ahead of myself again. I know it's a big jump to go from an obscure, elderly couple to the Christ whose arms were pinned to a cross, crying out on behalf of those he loves.

Or is it?

The truth is, Abraham did think he was going to have to sacrifice his son, but Hebrews 11:9 says he also believed that Isaac would somehow be raised from the dead. Turns out, it was a little too early for all that.

But it sure was a sign of things to come.

Chapter 5

TWINS, TRICKS, AND A TRAGIC HERO
Age of the Patriarchs

 My grandmother was one hundred years old when she died. She went seventeen days without food or water before she took her last breath. I was there when she passed away, and I'll tell you what—she died exactly how she lived, on her own stubborn Italian terms. Two weeks earlier, she was beating me in word jumbles. It's always incredibly hard to say goodbye to those we love, but, man, she really had a good, full life, and I'm grateful for that.

Sarah died at age 127. God bless the woman. Literally.

After she was gone, Abraham hopped on his "Tinder for Old Timers" app and started filling in some pretty legit credentials. He was on the prowl for a wife, but not for himself.

He just wanted to make sure his son Isaac ended up with the right woman, and he set some clear parameters in place for it. Mainly, she must not be a Canaanite (oh, if I just had a dollar for every time I've heard that) but, rather, a hometown girl. Abraham told one of his servants to head there and find the woman that Isaac was supposed to marry.

No pressure, guy whose name is never mentioned and who had to put his hand under Abraham's thigh and make a promise to find the right person. It's sort of like a borderline-creepy version of pinky-promising.

So Isaac is basically the Bachelor at this point. WHO WILL GET THE ROSE?

The servant left Canaan and headed to Nahor because it had the most awesome name. That's not true, but he did end up there, and if you take a look at the map, Nahor was in the vicinity of Haran. (Look back at your map on page 50. See how far he traveled? From Canaan back to Haran?) Of course God showed up the way he always does and led the servant right to the final contestant.

Lo and behold, not only was she going to be a bride, she was already part of the family! Her grandmother was the wife of one of Abraham's brothers. This made rehearsal dinner planning much easier; and also, everyone could sit on whichever side of the church they wanted. So I guess there was an upside.

Can we have a frank conversation? Let's think back to Adam and Eve. They had children. And then those children had children. And married those children? There were a lot of open-seating weddings, I'll just say it that way.

It's also worth noting that Abraham, back when he and his wife were younger, had a habit of telling people that Sarah was his sister. She was so beautiful that he thought other men would kill him if they knew the truth, just to get at her. Let's just say he wasn't *exactly* being dishonest. She was, in fact, his half-sister. Same dad, different mom. But, weird as this sounds for our culture and time, it was actually considered a whole lot better at this period in history to marry someone of your own kind than to marry an enemy, which was unthinkable.

Let's get back to Isaac's bride now, shall we?

Turns out the woman that the servant found was named Rebekah, and God made it abundantly clear that she was supposed to be Isaac's wife. Rebekah had a brother named

Laban—just keep that name in mind for later, too, because it'll add some dimension to the story. Anyway, Laban gave his sister permission to head back to Canaan with a man she'd never met, in order to marry a man she didn't know. How could that go wrong?

Well, the good news is that Isaac was smitten with her right away, and she became a great comfort to him as he was grieving the death of his mother.

All was well in Canaan, as they say.

Listen, you know better than to think it's going to stay calm, right?

Rebekah soon realized she was pregnant with twins. And they weren't exactly going to be the kind of kids you trust on playdates.

It's about to get real, sister.

SIBLING INSANITY

TWINS!!!!!!! What in the world would that feel like??? How crazy would it be to find out you were expecting two kids, then you went into preterm labor and had to be hospitalized and hooked up to an I.V. for ten weeks to fight for them to live! What? Is it just me?

Yep, *true story.* Identical twin girls (mirror image, actually) who are now eighteen as I write this paragraph. In fact, one of them is currently singing so loudly that I can't concentrate, so I'm just going to yell, "I.V.!" and hopefully she'll stop.

I'm glad my story diverges from Rebekah's at this point, because God had news about who these kids would be when they were born, and it wasn't exactly, ummmmm . . . IDEAL.

Here's what she already knew. They were especially rowdy in the womb, and Rebekah had a feeling there was something different about them. She was right. And God was about to confirm it:

> "Two nations are in your womb, and two
> peoples from within you shall be divided;
> the one shall be stronger than the other, the
> older shall serve the younger." (Gen. 25:23)

Esau was born first. With fiery red hair. Like, all over his body. Yummmmm. His younger brother Jacob came next, and it was clear his goal was to be first out. He had his hand wrapped tightly around Esau's foot, trying his best to pull him out of the way.

Incidentally (and I apologize to anyone who's given their child this name, because I love it myself too), the name Jacob means "heel-grabber." Seriously.

They turned out to be really different guys. Jacob was a mama's boy: quiet, reserved, not really great at manly stuff. You could also call him somewhat of a trickster. Esau, on the other hand, was a fantastic hunter and loved outdoorsy things.

I don't get the feeling, though, that Esau was particularly bright. At one point he came back from hunting and was so hungry that he agreed to give his birthright to Jacob in exchange for a bowl of soup (Gen. 25:29–34). And by "birthright," I mean his double inheritance as the technically older son. It would go to Jacob now, not him. I really hope it was good soup.

FROM ABRAHAM TO JACOB

Aw, Esau, all that hair probably affected your body heat. We might have done the same thing. Actually, no other human on Earth would have done something so stupid, but you probably did have a great personality.

Here's how it worked. This was a binding agreement. Like, you couldn't do take-backs or fingers-crossed or even ask your dad to fix it. It was a done deal. And the birthright thing wasn't the only blessing that someone inherited as a firstborn; there was also a blessing that designated one son as having "head of household" status after the father's death. It involved being prayed over with words of prophetic, prosperous vision for that son's future. So, which son had been lined up for that perk before this whole beef stew fiasco? Hungry Hairy, that's who.

Rebekah may have been a delightful bride/niece/cousin or whatever she was to Isaac, but she definitely had some strong opinions. In her mind, Jacob should have been the favorite all along. Hers wasn't just a subtle preference either, which is likely why Esau spent his time working out his frustration by killing things. Rebekah was happy about what happened with the stew (one blessing down), but she still wasn't satisfied. Jacob needed to get the other blessing too.

So she did what every mother does. She dressed Jacob in Esau's nasty clothes and strapped a hunk of goat hair around his arms. Time to go into papa Isaac's room and trick him into believing Jacob is his other son, Esau, which is not that complicated given that dad is ancient, blind, and about to die.

These are the things that don't make it into the wedding vows.

Jacob went in and promised his dad that he was Esau. At first Isaac didn't believe him, but the smell and the hair were pretty convincing, so he did exactly what Rebekah wanted him to do. He gave Jacob the blessing. Jacob was now two-for-two, and as you can imagine, Esau was not going to take this news well. You may be shocked to hear that Rebekah had a plan for this too. She was such a good (kind-of, not-really, conniving) mother. She said to Jacob:

> "My son, obey my voice. Arise, flee to Laban my brother in Haran and stay with him a while, until your brother's fury turns away— until your brother's anger turns away from you, and he forgets what you have done to him. Then I will send and bring you from there." (Gen. 27:43–45)

On days when I feel like a failure as a mother, I go back to this and feel consoled by the fact that I've never glued hair on one of my kids to take advantage of my dying spouse.

Now here's the thing. The fact that Jacob was kind of a scoundrel didn't change the truth: he was still the person God had decided to continue his covenant through. Remember? "The older shall serve the younger," right? Is it hard for you to imagine a person who'd done so many sneaky things could still be the one who was chosen by God? He'd taken advantage of family. He'd manipulated whatever he'd needed to manipulate in order to get what he wanted.

I guess what I'm saying is that I'm glad there are Jacobs in the Bible. The situations in my life are obviously different, but I've been all of the things Jacob was, and probably a million more. I've been selfish. I've been deceptive. I've heel-grabbed at the person whose lot I wanted in life. You? No? Good for you, liar. That's why this is one of my favorite stories in the Bible. God chooses and uses the most unlikely, unexpected, and undeserving people in the world. He can do anything with anyone. And I don't mean it in just a cutesy bumper-sticker way. He actually can. And he does.

Jacob is going to find this out in the most amazing way, but first we need to get him married. And then married again. And then, yeah, it'll be a little while before we get to the part I love most. But isn't it always that way with a good story?

FIELD OF DREAMS

Running for his life, Jacob tore out for Haran, praying his mother was right—that his uncle Laban would provide a place for him and protect him from his brother's wrath. But before he made it beyond the boundaries of Canaan, he stopped somewhere to spend the night. And in the dark of that evening, under a sky filled with too many stars to count, the Lord met him in a dream.

> Behold, there was a ladder set up on the earth, and the top of it reached to heaven. And behold, the angels of God were ascending and descending on it! (Gen. 28:12)

Have you ever heard of Jacob's ladder? If so, this story is where it comes from.

And just so you'll know, the "ladder" was not merely some abstract creation of Jacob's stressed-out subconscious. Know how I know?—because Jesus, many years later, told one of his followers not to be surprised someday to "see heaven opened, and the angels of God ascending and descending on the Son of Man" (John 1:51). "Son of Man," by the way, was one of Jesus' favorite titles for himself. In other words, *Jesus is the ladder.* Jesus is the One who makes it possible for fallen people on the earth to interact with the God of heaven.

And why does that matter in this Genesis moment? It matters because God was about to remind Jacob about the covenant he had made, the covenant he'd made with his grandfather Abraham, the covenant he'd made with his father Isaac—about "dust of the earth"—about north, south, east, and west—about how "in you and your offspring shall all the families of the earth be blessed" (Gen. 28:14).

> "Behold, I am with you and will keep you wherever you go, and I will bring you back to this land. For I will not leave you until I have done what I have promised you." (v. 15)

And Jesus, the ladder, was foreshadowed right there in the middle of it. In the middle of this promise. To Jacob. To his offspring.

To us.

I mean, that's amazing. Jacob was so shuddered by it that he renamed the place Bethel, meaning "house of God." It had previously been called Luz, a name that was sort of crying out for a refurbish anyway. I think it was just time for a change everywhere. And God, of course, knew it.

Now it's not as though Jacob was through making problems for the Lord to solve. I want to be real clear about that. He will prove himself a sinner yet, like all of us do. But also know this: God had started to change him. Like he changes us. We are changed by God's unchanging promises.

DESPERATE HOUSEWIVES

By Genesis 29, Jacob had gotten close to his final destination but decided to stop for a break at a community well. Good thing he did, because a Hallmark movie score had already begun. He met some guys who knew his uncle Laban, and as they were chatting, a beautiful woman approached the well, leading her sheep to water.

Here we go again—it's Laban's daughter, Rachel.

As you may have noticed, Jacob wasn't the kind of guy who waited around to get what he wanted. So he grabbed Rachel's hand and kissed it. The music was changing.

And I know what you're asking because I was haunted by the same question: *Did the sheep get their water?* There are so many mysteries in the Bible. We just need to accept the fact that we won't know everything.

Jacob wasted no time in asking for Rachel as his wife, and he promised Laban seven years of work in exchange for her hand in marriage. Let me be clear. It wasn't a "get married now and hang out here for seven years after that." It was a "you now have ample amount of time to put together a registry."

I mean, seven years is a long time.

Especially when it turns out the way it did. Wait for it. WAIT. Because the trickster is about to get tricked.

Jacob married his bride. Except, not exactly. We don't know if it was the dim lighting or the cocktails, but let's just say he somehow didn't realize (UNTIL THE NEXT MORNING! AND, YES, I HAVE QUESTIONS!) that Laban had actually given him Rachel's sister Leah instead of Rachel.

Leah was the older one, so by rights she should've been married first. At least, that's the way her dad saw it. And this was the perfect opportunity to do it, because who knew when another groom might come along and want Rachel's sister. She wasn't, umm . . . she wasn't as much of a looker as Rachel. In fact, it's possible she literally couldn't "look" as well as Rachel could because something was physically wrong with her eyes. As in maybe being cross-eyed? We don't know for sure. The Bible describes Rachel as having a beautiful face and figure but says Leah's "eyes were weak" (Gen. 29:17).

Awwwww. The poor girl had been thrown into a marriage knowing she wasn't the one the groom wanted, and also the bridesmaids spent a lot of money on those dresses. Don't worry—they'll be reused in a hot second.

Laban told Jacob he could marry Rachel, too, if he promised another seven years of work. Good news, though! (Well, not for Leah.) He could have Rachel in seven *days* if he agreed to Laban's terms. And so began the second half of Jacob's "work-for-wives" program.

I'm sure Leah had never felt so special in her life.

I kid, but the truth is, *she* was the special one (according to the values of the time period she lived in) because she could bear children, and Rachel was barren. But it was all purposeful: "The LORD saw that Leah was hated," the Bible says, and so "he opened her womb" (Gen. 29:31).

First, she had a son named Reuben. Then came Simeon. After that, Levi.

The meaning of each of the names she gave them, in the original language, spoke to her irrational hope that Jacob would finally be inclined to love her, perhaps even love her best, because of the sons she was giving him that Rachel wasn't. But I don't suppose it worked. Because by the time her fourth son was born, she called him Judah, meaning "praise," saying simply, "This time I will praise the LORD" (Gen. 29:35).

I want you to read that last part again because it affects the entire scope of Scripture and the narrative of what's to come.

Praise the Lord, she said. *My hope is not in man. It is in the Lord himself.*

Jacob would have many more sons before he was through, but only one would hold the distinct honor of having Jesus in his lineage. You may have guessed which one it was. Yep, Judah. So beautiful, isn't it?

Praise the Lord, she said.

And so do we.

All right, so Leah was now secure in God. All was well, right? Nope. Enter angry sister. Rachel, well—she wasn't exactly as excited about her nephews as she should have been. She wanted her own child.

> When Rachel saw that she bore Jacob no children, she envied her sister. She said to Jacob, "Give me children, or I shall die!" (Gen. 30:1)

A little dramatic, no?

But it's okay—because Jacob was about to take a cue from his grandfather Abraham and find a work-around, all at Rachel's bidding. I mean, I guess she was a problem solver. But I can't say this is the way I would have done it. She told Jacob to have sex with her maidservant.

And again, a husband sacrifices himself on behalf of his loving wife. All he wants in this world is to make her happy by bringing her another woman's baby.

Okay. Well, anyway, he did exactly what Rachel asked him to do, and he ended up with two more sons through her maidservant (named Bilhah). Leah, though, was not going to be outdone, so she had her own maidservant jump in the circus ring as well (Zilpah, in case you're looking for some inspiration). Just like that, two more boys were born. And seeing her maidservant get involved in the action, Leah decided she wasn't ready to stop having babies herself, so she continued to outfox beautiful Rachel by having two more boys. And then, one girl. Welcome to the family, Dinah.

After all of this, the Bible has some great words that will lead to a lot more great stories. You ready?

> Then God remembered Rachel, and God listened to her and opened her womb. She

conceived and bore a son and said, "God has taken away my reproach." (Gen. 30:22–23)

You may have heard of this son, Joseph, or at least his statement piece, his coat of many colors. But if not, don't worry. We'll get there soon. He was the eleventh boy. These people were nothing if not fertile and hearty.

We'll hear a lot more from Joseph by the time we reach the end of this chapter. But I doubt you'll be surprised to know, even though he was officially Jacob's eleventh son, he was really number one in his father's heart, simply because he was Rachel's. Don't think Jacob hadn't been trained well in playing favorites.

So here's the count of everything at this point: two wives, eleven boys, one daughter. And because of this growing brood, along with all the livestock and so forth that he'd accumulated through the years, Jacob's footprint was taking up a lot of space now on Laban's property. He was feeling cramped, stifled, and ready to be his own boss. He told Laban that he was going to round up his family and take off for another spot. Laban was not exactly pumped about this situation, which led to Jacob's midnight escape.

I can't even get my kids in the car without at least two mental breakdowns, a missing left shoe, and three more trips back inside for things they forgot. So basically what I'm saying is that I'm impressed. They were heading back to Canaan. (And this is where you realize, having just read of their destination, you completely recognize the sound of that place and you understand exactly where I'm talking about. And I tip my hat to you. See? You've got this.)

Is there anything else you can think of that might be placed in the "unfinished business" category, as far as what this return trip might involve? Yeahhhhhhhhh . . . Esau was closing in on Jacob, and he wasn't coming alone.

No time to get anyone else pregnant, dude. You need to hustle.

BATTLE ROYALE

In the twenty years or so since Jacob had been gone, Esau had left home too and settled with his growing family to the east of Canaan in a rugged, mountainous region that would come to be known as Edom. (Esau, according to Genesis 36:9, was considered the "father of the Edomites.") So, for Jacob, transporting his family and possessions by main road into Canaan meant exposing them to a stretch of his brother Esau's land, which, as you can imagine, wasn't the safest option. But what if Esau had calmed down? I mean, it was worth a shot, because this route was the best way to travel, and there were 45,567 children in tow, asking how much longer it was going to be.

Jacob sent in spies to get some information, and this is what they told him:

> "We came to your brother Esau, and he is coming to meet you, and there are four hundred men with him." (Gen. 32:6)

This is exactly what Jacob was hoping for, *am I right?* He thought quickly on his feet and decided to split his crew into two groups. That way, Esau and his men could kill just half of them, and the other half would escape.

> JACOB: Okay, everyone. Listen up. We're going to form two groups. All the hot wives and calm kids, come with me, please.

Then Jacob did the only thing he could think to do. He prayed:

> "O God of my father Abraham and God of my father Isaac, O LORD who said to me,

'Return to your country and to your kindred, that I may do you good,' I am not worthy of the least of all the deeds of steadfast love and all the faithfulness that you have shown to your servant, for with only my staff I crossed this Jordan, and now I have become two camps. Please deliver me from the hand of my brother, from the hand of Esau, for I fear him, that he may come and attack me, the mothers with the children."
(Gen. 32:9–11)

Let's pause for a second. Jacob was asking for God's favor. How interesting—because I think we'd all agree, based on Jacob's behavior so far, there would be no reason for God to extend any mercy to him.

And if I were asked to put all of Scripture into a sentence, that might be close to where I would land. We deserve nothing. We have sinned over and over, and we have the audacity to ask the Lord for forgiveness and favor. Yet he loves us enough to do just that. It's the upside-down economy of the gospel. And it'll make more sense as we get farther down the road.

Jacob remembered the promise God had made to his family:

"You said, 'I will surely do you good, and make your offspring as the sand of the sea, which cannot be numbered for multitude.'"
(v. 12)

God will never break his promises, and we can lean on those promises whenever we're up against fear, sadness, and desperation. We can know what he has said to us, and we can repeat those words in prayer to remind ourselves that he is a good Father. *Like Jacob did.*

Remember when I told you I was going to get to one of my favorite stories in the Bible? Well, here we are. As the shadows of that day began to lengthen, Jacob escorted his wives, his servants, and his children across a ford in the Jabbok River, a bit north and east of Canaan. He found a place where he could be alone, and there he had an encounter that would forever change him and the rest of history.

As the Bible puts it, "A man wrestled with him until the breaking of the day" (Gen. 32:24). And who was the man? And why was Jacob wrestling with him? It's not the answer you would expect.

Jacob was in a match with God himself. (In case you're wondering, *Wait, is this another one of those "theophany" things you mentioned a while back?*, you'd be 100-percent correct, except some people call this particular instance a *Christophany*, where the pre-incarnated Christ shows up! WILD, right?)

Let's state the obvious here: I think we know who had the advantage. But Jacob refused to let go.

I can't imagine the amount of sweat dripping, the tears burning, and the muscles aching, hours before this tiring ordeal was finished. But finally, while they wrestled, the Lord touched Jacob's hip socket, pulling it out of place. I wonder if it had to do with the way Jacob had tried to *pull* Esau back when they were being born? That was the beginning of the pattern of life he'd continued up until this moment. Remember, Jacob pulled at Esau's leg because he wanted to go first, to walk ahead of his brother. He was constantly using his own strength and cunning to enter into blessing. He wanted blessing and approval and the status of being a favored one so badly that he'd grab at it any way he could—by trickery, strategy, or running ahead of danger. Heel-grabbing since the day of his birth, he was Jacob. He'd always been Jacob.

But God asked him a question here. And believe me, you'll look back on it at some point and understand why I cry when I read it. At daybreak, God told Jacob to release him, but Jacob refused: "I will not let you go unless you bless me" (v. 26). He already had his father Isaac's blessings—the ones he stole, the ones he didn't deserve, the ones that reminded him every day that he was a manipulator. And yet, here he was, wrestling with his Father God, asking for even more. A blessing he had no right to have.

"What is your name?" God asked him (v. 27).

It may seem like a strange question (and I assume you're aware of the fact that he knew the answer), but it's monumental.

"Jacob," he answered.

Everything, *everything* about Jacob's identity was wrapped up in that name. His reputation. His sin. His lies and twisted plans. "Jacob" was who he'd always been.

I know how easy it is for me to feel the same way, as I hear myself speaking my name. The only way I can identify myself is as a fraud, a cheater who somehow slipped through the system and convinced people she was more than she believed she was.

But then God said this to him:

> "Your name shall no longer be called Jacob,
> but Israel, for you have striven with God
> and with men, and have prevailed." (v. 28)

For my entire growing-up life, I was teased about my last name: Battiato (pronounced baht-e-AH-toe). Sounds a lot like "body auto." Or, less charitably, "body odor." But it wasn't just the cruel nickname quality of it that made my early days of life painful for me. Suffice it to say, there was plenty about my schooldays that left me carrying baggage I wanted to put behind me, things I so deeply desired to forget.

A few years ago, during a trip with my family, I found myself back in my hometown. And as my husband, my girls, and I drove around, we ended up near my old high school. It wasn't a place I necessarily wanted to revisit, but I guess I was just curious about what it looked like after so many years. Not just physically. I think I wanted to know how I would see it now.

The doors were locked, but I cupped my hands around my face and could still make out the rows of lockers, the huge staircase, and the edge of the cafeteria. I could give you memories of every square inch of that place. Most of them are shadowed, just the way they looked at that moment. I stood there as long as I could, but it only took a few minutes of memories to repel me from the glass.

I can't tell you exactly what made me do it, but after I had taken a few steps away, I turned back to the door. I was far enough away to see my reflection in it, and the woman I could see on this side was not the girl I had known on the other. It was as though the Lord whispered into my ear, "You're not who you used to be, Angie. *This* is who I see now. *This* person. *This* woman. You don't need to keep looking down those old hallways any longer, trying to change what they reveal. You're a new creation now."

I've given you a new name.

And that is just what God did with Jacob.
He named him Israel.

"Jacob" was no longer. He had striven with God and prevailed. He'd now been given another blessing, another name, and another hope for what was to come.

As the sun rose, there stood a man who'd been called to remember the night. To remember the blessings, the promises, and the name that would forevermore be spoken as part of the greatest story of all time.

Israel.

The one who carried a limp for the rest of his life after he left the place where God had broken him in order to heal him.

THE NUMBER TWELVE

As it turns out, Esau had let go of his old grudges. In fact, he embraced Jacob (now Israel, remember) and it turned out to be a peaceful encounter.

I wonder if Jacob brought stew for old times' sake.

After their reunion, Israel moved along with his family, passing by Bethel (where he'd had the dream about the ladder) and worked his way toward a town called Ephrath, better known to us as Bethlehem. They were known for their chili cook-offs and goat pageants, so it seemed like a natural choice. That's not at all true, but I've been writing for a long time, and it seemed funny in the moment.

Have you noticed it's been like a whole page since we last had a new baby in the fold? Well, break out the gender reveal decorations, because Rachel is about to see some more blue.

Benjamin—the twelfth boy born to Israel.

But his name would never be spoken without being tied to one of the worst moments in Israel's life. Because as he was born, his mother died.

Now there were twelve.

Twelve sons given to Jacob.

Twelve sons given to the man whom God renamed Israel.

Yes—the twelve tribes of Israel, which would form the living skeleton of the nation.

Forgive me if that's already obvious to you, just—it wasn't always so obvious to me.

Now stick with me for a second because this is going to get a little tricky. Eventually everyone born of the Israelite race throughout Scripture would identify themselves by

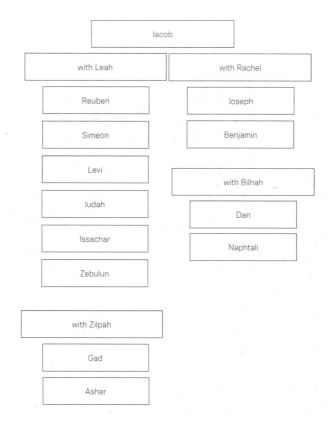

SONS OF JACOB

the given line—the "tribe"—their ancestors descended from. Even way over in the New Testament, when Paul gave a quick bio sketch of his life, he listed the high points as being "circumcised on the eighth day, of the people of Israel, of the tribe of Benjamin" (Phil. 3:5). BECAUSE DON'T WE ALL HAVE THAT ON OUR RÉSUMÉ?

A Jew's individual heritage, within their *corporate* heritage, was linked to their tribal connection. And soon when we come to the part of the story where God delivers his people from Egyptian slavery and establishes them in

Canaan, we'll see him apportion the Promised Land by tribal allotment. Each tribe will get a piece of it.

But even though we do end up with a total of twelve ancestral groupings, there's a little wrinkle in there that's worth mentioning, to avoid confusion.

This is going to look like a lot of information, so don't get discouraged if you can't quite make sense of it yet.

The tribe of Levi was tasked with being the nation's priests. And since the Lord himself was considered the priests' "inheritance," they weren't assigned any physical land to call their own. Nor was Joseph, though not because he wasn't special. He was *so* special, in fact, that each of his two sons (Manasseh and Ephraim) received a region of land named specifically for them.

So that's how—when we subtract Levi and Joseph from the land distribution, but then add Manasseh and Ephraim we get back up to twelve.

If I haven't made this point clear enough, or if you still don't quite understand the details, no biggie. All I'm trying to show you is why the twelve *sons* of Israel and the *tribes* of Israel are slightly different from each other.

None of them, though, was quite like Joseph.

THE STORY GOES SOUTH

Abraham, Isaac, and Jacob. And now his twelve strapping sons. Taken together, these men are what's known in Scripture as the *patriarchs,* the founding fathers of Israel. But chief among the twelve sons is undoubtedly Joseph, whose part of the story fills out the remaining chapters of Genesis.

We know he was his father's unapologetic favorite—as did everyone else, including his brothers. In fairness, though, Joseph didn't exactly try too hard to play it down. He made a point of reminding them about his special, elevated status at every opportunity, like when his dad gave him that stylish "robe of many colors" (Gen. 37:3) to signify

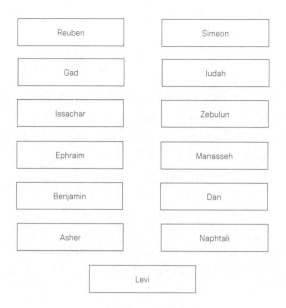

Reuben	Simeon
Gad	Judah
Issachar	Zebulun
Ephraim	Manasseh
Benjamin	Dan
Asher	Naphtali
Levi	

TRIBES OF ISRAEL

his unparalleled importance, and Joseph strutted around wearing it. Or when he reported to them on the details of dreams that came to him in his sleep, where his brothers played the role of bowing down to his superiority.

Needless to say, they got really tired of him, so they did what any of us would do. They threw him down a well, sold him into slavery, and slaughtered a goat so they could smear blood over his jacket to prove to their father that he was dead.

Goats were really getting the raw end of the deal, weren't they?

So who exactly did they sell him to? A band of Ishmaelite traders. (Ishmaelites? Hmm, where have we heard that name before?)

I doubt this moment made it into the family's scrapbook.

Jacob was devastated. He'd lost his favorite wife and his favorite son. He slipped into a period of mourning in which no one could comfort him, having no idea that the story wasn't what it appeared to be.

For this next part, I request your audience participation as we cover the next several years of Joseph's life:

- Joseph's captors took him south to Egypt and sold him as a slave. (Boo!)
- His owner, a guy named Potiphar, came to like and depend on him. (Yay!)
- But then Potiphar's wife falsely accused him of raping her. (Boo!)
- And he was thrown into prison for a crime he didn't do. (Boo!!)
- Where he stayed for a really, really, really long time. (Boo!!!)
- But while there, he interpreted dreams for two guys. (Cool.)
- Eventually, his reputation reached the pharaoh. (Wow.)
- And after he interpreted a dream for him . . . (Really?)
- He was made second-in-command over all of Egypt.

Can you say, PLOT TWIST?

The dreams that Joseph interpreted for the Egyptian pharaoh warned about an upcoming famine. There would be seven years where crops would be plentiful, followed by seven years of drought. So now was the time to gather up stuff and get ready for the day when they would need it.

But if this strategy seems brilliant on Joseph's part, God is the one whose brilliance should actually amaze us, because as many as three generations earlier, God had given Abraham a bit of insight he couldn't possibly have understood. He told him his offspring would end up being relocated to a foreign land, would then become treated like slaves, and would be "afflicted for four hundred years. But I will bring judgment on the nation that they serve, and afterward they shall come out with great possessions" (Gen. 15:13–14).

We'll come back to this prophecy later, but it's a good time to start unpacking it now. Because while the impending famine seemed like breaking news to Joseph and the Egyptians, God had been writing and reporting on this story for years. Do you see that the famine was his chosen tool for getting Abraham's offspring transported to Egypt, where they would settle and prosper because Joseph would provide for them? I've been in plenty of "famines," and I can look back now and see the way God provided. In the moment? Not so much. And though it eventually led, sadly, to many years of hard slavery for the Israelites, God had a spectacular plan in place. We'll get to that in the next chapter, but here's where it starts:

> When Jacob learned that there was grain for sale in Egypt, he said to his sons, "Why do you look at one another? . . . Go down and buy grain for us there, that we may live and not die." (Gen. 42:1–2)

Off they go. Or ten of them anyway. Jacob chose to hold back his youngest son, Benjamin, fearing something might happen to him. He didn't want to lose Rachel's other son the way he'd lost the first one. The ten who went, however, found themselves face to face with the person in charge of selling grain to down-and-out travelers coming to Egypt in search of help. They didn't notice the family resemblance. But Joseph did.

What are the chances of your brothers throwing you into a well and selling you into slavery, only to be standing in front of you asking for help? I mean, this is some good stuff right here.

I would not have been as kind as Joseph, but that's probably because I'm a terrible person and I really liked that outfit.

- First, Joseph accused them of being spies. Played hardball.
- Bled them for information, and they sang like scared canaries.
- Then he put them all together in jail for three days. Because, why not?
- Said they weren't going anywhere until they got their little brother there.
- Finally decided to hold one of them hostage and send the rest of them home.
- And what's more, he put their money back in their bags to make it look like they'd stolen it.

They returned to their father, explaining that they'd been found guilty of theft, and the only way they could be found innocent was to return with their youngest brother, Benjamin—their father's favorite living son. They would starve if they didn't do what the man had asked. They had no choice but to return. *All* of them.

When they got back to Egypt, Joseph arranged for them to be brought to his house, which scared them to death. He asked them if their father was alive, and they told him that he was. Joseph locked eyes with Benjamin, and was so overcome with emotion that he had to leave the room to compose himself.

He also left the room because (are you ready for this?) it was considered an abomination for Egyptians to eat with Jews. But he set them up with a nice dinner and told his staff to seat them around the table by birth order.

Clever, Joseph. Very clever. I wonder if they gave him a placeholder.

Doesn't matter. He's about to show up, and he's coming in HOT.

He told his servant to notify the boys with some news that was sure to bless them. I mean, at this point they had to be wondering what the heck this guy was doing. Joseph, however, knew exactly what he was doing. He was determined to see his dad, and there was only one way to get him there: keep Benji as collateral.

This was not going to go well. I mean, losing both of their father's faves was less than ideal. Judah piped up and begged Joseph to keep him there instead. (WHERE WERE YOU WHEN THE WHOLE FAKE BLOOD THING HAPPENED, JUDE???) It was a no-go.

But, wow—Judah was willing to sacrifice himself in place of another. Not only that, but let's quickly recall who these kiddos actually were. He was Leah's spiritual-breakthrough child who was offering to sacrifice himself for Benjamin, the only other son (other than Joseph) born to Rachel and Jacob. Tensions between these two sides of the family had been mounting for years, and now we see one of them offering himself *for his enemy*. The underdog giving himself up for the beloved.

Sounds like another Man who would come from the tribe of Judah.

Apparently, that's all Joseph could take. Knowing his father was alive, knowing his youngest brother was standing right there next to him, he couldn't swallow his emotions anymore, and his voice echoed throughout the home that, under more normal circumstances, would never have been his home.

"I am Joseph," he said.

And with those words, disbelief silenced the brothers. Fear overwhelmed them. Shock tangled their thoughts as they tried to comprehend what was happening.

This man in power—the one who held their fate in his hands—was their flesh and blood. The one they were so jealous of—the one they'd sent away as a slave—now had them at his mercy.

But it wouldn't end the way we might expect, because Joseph wasn't after revenge. He loved them too much to repay them with hatred. Like so many others in the insane story of his family, God had changed him. "It was not you who sent me here, but God," he said (Gen. 45:8). Or as he would put it later, after Jacob had come to join them, after all of them were together again as a family: "You meant evil against me, but God meant it for good" (Gen. 50:20).

It's why an aged Jacob, unlike how his father Isaac had done, could call all twelve of his sons together, without favoritism, and speak blessing over each one of them. The old deceiver had finally given up his confidence in con games, believing he could simply trust God's word concerning his family's future.

As Jacob neared the end of his life, he asked to be taken to Canaan to be buried, to be placed in the same cave as Isaac, Rebekah, Abraham, and Sarah. But that was just a glimpse of what God was really doing. Yes, Jacob's request would be honored, and years later, Joseph's bones would be brought home as well—out of Egypt and back to Canaan.

The Lord, he said, would someday bring this entire covenant nation up out of Egypt and would plant them again in "the land that he swore to Abraham, to Isaac, and to Jacob" (Gen. 50:24), and to the thousands upon thousands who would make up their family tree.

Because God's people aren't made for Egypt.

They're made to live in the land of promise.

Chapter 6

HELLO, WE WERE
JUST LEAVING
The Exodus

 Can you believe it? We finally made it out of Genesis, and it only took us five chapters. I assure you it's been time well spent, though. As we keep trucking, I'll make sure to mention it when we're looking at a quote or piece of storyline that points back to something we've already studied, and I think you're going to be surprised at how differently you read them after you make those connections.

So here we are in the second book of the Bible: Exodus, because, well, it's centered on the exodus of the Israelites from Egypt.

Here's the thing. It was all good at first when that little band of Israelites was living out in the country, but things started to take a turn as they began to increase their population. The last thing the Egyptians wanted was a group of people who could possibly overthrow them. Generations had gone by since Jacob arrived with no more than "seventy persons" (Exod. 1:5), including sons and their wives and their children and servants. So it's not like they started out as a powerhouse group of people; it's just that they were fertile. I mean, WHOA FERTILE. Scripture says it more eloquently: "They were fruitful and increased greatly; they multiplied and grew exceedingly strong, so that the land was filled with them" (v. 7).

But Joseph knew them, so they weren't really worried about anything going wrong. You may have picked up on this by now: things don't always go as planned.

> Now there arose a new king over Egypt, who did not know Joseph. (v. 8)

Okay, let's do some memory work. Do you remember how the descendants of Noah's three sons had fanned out over the adjoining continents? And how the family line of Ham drifted south to occupy what later became Egypt? And how the children of Shem—the Semites—settled in the region where Abraham's family came from? Remember all that? Sure you do. Feel free to head back to your maps as a reminder.

Combine that information with this next bit of information that I got from the *Encyclopedia Britannica*.[4] Sometime around the eighteenth-century BC, a Semitic group of people known as the Hyksos went down south and conquered Egypt. A couple hundred years later though, the Thebans, a group of native Egyptians (i.e., Hamites) rebelled against the Semitic Hyksos and threw them out of power.

So? What?

The "so what" is that Joseph's years in Egypt—which span the last ten or twelve chapters of Genesis—occurred during the Hyksos period. In other words, the pharaoh who promoted Joseph to second-in-command was a fellow Semite. But in the hundreds of years that followed, during which Israel's offspring "increased greatly" and "grew exceedingly strong," a new, homegrown pharaoh came to power in Egypt—one who "did not know Joseph" and, therefore, felt no loyalty or kinship toward the Israelites or to the people they'd become.

Worse than that, he became terribly suspicious of them. He felt, because of their immense and growing size, they represented a possible threat. If war were to break out, for instance, and the Israelites decided to align themselves with an invading army, they could pose a considerable force against the Egyptians, operating from right there on the inside. That's something Pharaoh certainly didn't want to see happen. So before any more time could pass—before the people of Israel could grow any more numerous—the Egyptian powers-that-be decided to intervene.

The first wave of action taken against them was to make them a slave class. The Egyptians "set taskmasters over them to afflict them with heavy burdens" (Exod. 1:11). They took them away from freely pursuing their own lives and interests and put them to work on federalized construction projects. And yet "the more they were oppressed," the Bible says, "the more they multiplied and the more they spread abroad" (v. 12).

So, the pharaoh made it worse, becoming even *more* ruthless in subduing the Israelites. The Bible says he broke their spirits through "hard service, in mortar and brick, and in all kinds of work in the field" (v. 14). He even went so far as to order the Hebrew midwives (Jewish people at that time were known as "Hebrews") to commit infanticide on any male child who was born to an Israelite woman. He apparently didn't care if the *daughters* lived, since they wouldn't grow up to staff an army against him, but the baby boys were to be smothered before they took their first breaths.

These midwives, though—and I love this—"feared God and did not do as the king of Egypt commanded them" (v. 17). They resisted. They wouldn't do it. And when asked about it, they told Pharaoh the Hebrew women were "not like the Egyptian women, for they are vigorous and give birth before the midwife comes to them" (v. 19).

Niiiiiiccccceeeee.

So, does that all make sense? The Jews (Hebrews) were becoming a supposed threat to the Egyptians, so they were going to need to be subdued.

This, then, is your context for the book of Exodus, the bitter background that sets the stage for the next chapter in the Bible's story.

And as we spread it out before us for observation, we introduce the next piece of thread into the fabric, the next needle to become a thorn in Pharaoh's side.

Moses.

PATTERNS FORMING

> Now a man from the house of Levi went and took as his wife a Levite woman. The woman conceived and bore a son, and . . .
> (Exod. 2:1–2)

Waittttttt a minute. We've heard that name before, haven't we? *Levi.* Okay, who was his father? How many brothers did he have? What was the role of the Levites in the priesthood of the nation of Israel?

So this passage is telling us that a man from the house of Levi would have a child named Moses. And he would be a man who would spend the better part of his life intervening between the people and their God—almost like, yeah, a priest.

IT ALMOST SEEMS LIKE PART OF A PLAN, DOESN'T IT???

But back now to the babies.

Meet Jochebed—the Levite woman with the terrible name and the amazing son. And trust me, Moses is going to have one of the most interesting stories in Scripture..

Moses was born under this death sentence that we've seen, where Hebrew boys were to be killed instantly by the presiding midwives. When that didn't work, Pharaoh told his own citizens just to snatch up any Hebrew baby boys they could get their hands on and fling them into the Nile River. But Jochebed couldn't bear to part with her newborn son, so she hid him at home for three months. I think we can imagine how hard it would be to hide a wriggly, screaming baby for much longer than that. Soon she was faced with a secret that was simply unsustainable. So, she crafted a waterproof basket large enough to lay her son safely inside and strategically positioned it in the reeds along the riverbank where it would attract curiosity.

Moses' sister Miriam walked alongside the basket as it floated, hidden behind the brush while praying he would be rescued. And again we see the providence of God. The first person to see Moses was the daughter of Pharaoh, and better than that, she decided she would keep him and raise him as an Egyptian in the most powerful house in the land.

But the baby needed to be nursed until he was weaned, and—WHAT ARE THE CHANCES?—Miriam volunteered her mother. So Moses got to go back home for a little while before he was eventually returned to the pharaoh's house. And despite the fact that she wasn't able to keep him, I'm sure Jochebed was relieved that he would be in an environment where he was well cared for, fed, and loved.

It's really important to pay attention to the patterns of Scripture, and one of the patterns in Moses' life, for example, involves *water*. At several key points throughout his life, Moses experienced God's mastery over this natural resource. It started when Moses was born, when he was spared from being drowned as a Hebrew baby (that's #1) and then was later drawn out of the water by Pharaoh's daughter (that's #2). Sit tight. More about water coming later.

So if it suits your style of study, you might actually want to keep a little notebook nearby whenever you're reading the Bible from now on, and write different themes that you notice as you come to them (like the ones I've been telling you about). Maybe it's sibling rivalry or the way dreams play into stories. Maybe it's goat hair. The options are endless. That way, as you read, you can jot them down, and you'll soon start to see the way themes continue to repeat themselves in Scripture.

While we're on the topic of patterns, let's mention one that's really descriptive of the cycle of relationship between God and his people in the Bible. It happens again and again like this.

- They cry out to him.
- He hears their cry for help.
- He remembers his covenant.
- He moves to rescue them.

To be clear, "remember" doesn't insinuate that he forgot; it simply means he acted on his promises.

All right, smarty. Go ahead and read this next part. Maybe it's something you've seen before, but without the context, it may have just looked like details that didn't connect to anything. How about now?

> The people of Israel groaned because of their slavery and cried out for help. Their cry for rescue from slavery came up to God. And God heard their groaning, and God remembered his covenant with Abraham, with Isaac, and with Jacob. God saw the people of Israel—and God knew. (Exod. 2:23–25)

See? You know all about those places and names now. I mean, you just handled Exodus 2:23–25. What is there in the world that you can't take on after that?

The answer is nothing. So let's jump back into Moses' life. Things are about to get crazy over here.

A BURNING DESIRE

By faith Moses, when he was grown up, refused to be called the son of Pharaoh's daughter. (Heb. 11:24)

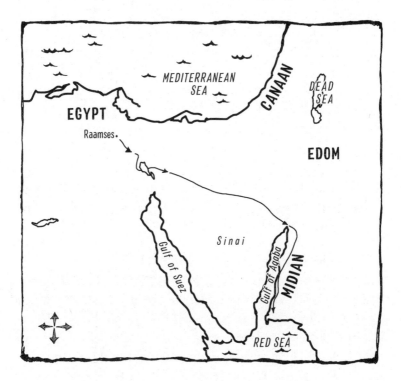

MOSES RUNS FROM PHARAOH

Let me stop for a second before we move on. This might not mean too much to you right now, but that last verse doesn't show up anywhere near where we are. In fact, it doesn't show up until the New Testament in a book called Hebrews. Why on earth would it be called that? Yep, because of the Hebrews we're hanging out with right here, before we've even gotten to the third book of the Bible. Because it's all one sto . . . sorry. I'm just making sure you don't miss any of this.

And now that we're caught up in Egypt, see if you can guess why Moses wouldn't want to be called the son of Pharaoh's daughter? You've got it—because he was a Hebrew.

In what was not the finest moment of his life, Moses once came upon a Hebrew man being beaten by an Egyptian. He decided to kill him, bury him, and jet to Midian to be a shepherd because that's what his travel agent recommended. Eventually he and his new Midianite wife settled in for a nice long life with their kiddos.

End of story, right?

You know better.

Remember in Genesis when Adam and Eve tried to hide? It was, what's the word . . . unsuccessful? Well, talk about patterns. A guy like Moses might be able to hide from Pharaoh's folks, but as it turns out, God has pretty phenomenal radar.

So here's where we are in the Bible, just to give you a little bird's-eye view: the Israelites are still enslaved to the Egyptians, but God has promised them a land that will be flowing with milk and honey, a safe place where they'll no longer be mistreated and despised. It's theirs by covenant. And guess who he chose to bring the Israelites out of Egypt so they could go to that land? Who knew the tiny baby floating in the reeds would grow up to be the rescuer of his people?

There's a famous scene in Exodus 3 where God appeared to him in a *theophany*. (Remember that word?) He did it through a burning bush. Notice how the Lord introduced himself:

> "I am the God of your father, the God of Abraham, the God of Isaac, and the God of Jacob." (v. 6)

WAITTTTTTT . . . why on earth would God be throwing out a reminder of who Moses' ancestors were? I mean, Moses probably already knew that, right? But God gave it to him as a reminder of the promise made to Abraham, the promise that had been carried all the way through the generations and had now trickled down to him.

Hey, Moses? You're the guy. Set down your staff because God's about to set a bush on fire. And then? You're going to lead all of your people out of Egypt and try to escape everyone who's wanting to kill you. Oh, and also, you'll be landlocked, but we'll get to that part later. It'll be fine. Plus, God said he's going to make Pharaoh mad—mad enough that he'll refuse the whole thing and will go all crazy on you. *Enjoy your brunch, Moses.*

But this is a huge moment here. Don't miss it.

As the Exodus story progresses, we learn that Moses' relationship with God grew to become one in which the Lord spoke with him "face to face, as a man speaks to his friend" (Exod. 33:11). They would one day possess a special closeness, unlike what anyone else experienced with God at that time. But not yet. As Moses came across the bush that God set on fire (subtle), we see him trembling and trying to back away from his assignment.

You've got this whole thing wrong, God. I'm a nobody. I will fail at all of it. So while I appreciate your thoughtful pyrotechnics, I am going to graciously back out. Byeeeeeee . . .

But, no, that wasn't the plan. With Moses standing there on holy ground, God told him to take off his shoes. Then God did something beautiful. And unprecedented.

He told Moses his name.

God has a name?

Indeed. I mean, he's "God," naturally. But that's more of a description, a category. What we learn at the burning bush is God's actual name, his covenant name.

One way of saying his name, he told Moses, is "I AM WHO I AM" (Exod. 3:14)—the eternal, self-existent God who has always been, will always be, and needs no one's help to be who he is. "I AM" is his name. But his name is also represented (in verse 15) by four Hebrew consonants that translate to our YHWH, known in theological circles as the *tetragrammaton* (s'up, Scrabble), meaning "four letters."

Centuries ago, English scholars ascribed a pronunciation to these letters—*Jehovah*—although most people today agree it's more accurately pronounced *Yahweh*. Actually though, reverence for God's name led to the Jewish practice of not speaking or writing his name at all. That's why in many translations, the unspeakable letters YHWH have been replaced by the Hebrew word *Adonai,* translated as "Lord." And so in your Bible—to show that the word "Lord" is a stand-in for God's given name (YHWH)—it appears in small caps, like this:

LORD

More than six thousand times.

Did you ever, like me, look at one of those six thousand instances of the word "LORD" in the Old Testament and wonder, "Why the small capital letters?" Now you know.

And now Moses knew it too. As Yahweh told him, "Say this to the people of Israel, 'The LORD'"—there it is again—"'has sent me to you.' This is my name forever, and thus I am to be remembered throughout all generations" (Exod. 3:15). And so when Moses told them the Lord had appeared to him and had seen the hardship they were under, God said they would listen. They would recognize their deliverer by his name. What a personal, powerful demonstration of his covenant for the people of Israel.

But things were about to get quite personal and powerful for the *Egyptians* as well. That's because Pharaoh, as predicted, was a definite no-go on Moses' request for leading the Israelites on a "three days' journey into the wilderness" to make sacrifice to their God (Exod. 5:3). *Sounds like a party, no?* No, that's not the way Pharaoh saw it: *You may not leave with your friends, Moses, you may not go have some wilderness party. This discussion is over. Go outside and see if there's anything in flames for you to play with.*

God got down to business to prove to Pharaoh he wasn't messing around. He sent ten plagues. One of them involved turning the Egyptians' water into blood (mark that down as win #3 in the water category), as well as swarms of gnats, swarms of flies, death of livestock, painful boils, fiery hail, hordes of locusts, and three days of total darkness. Plus, of course, everybody's favorite . . .

Frogs. For some reason, the plague of frogs is the one that still freaks people out the most, although its effect on the Egyptians was more than just the creepy, slimy, fear factor. Each of the plagues was a deliberate attack against one of the many nature gods these pagan people worshipped. So frogs were really important because they were considered sacred in their culture during this time period and were not to be killed. The Egyptians worshipped a frog-headed god that represented fertility. So when Yahweh allowed thousands of frogs to die in these people's homes, he was reminding them that he alone is the one true God.

After nine plagues, Pharaoh still had not relented. Hear me tell you this: the tenth plague would be one of the most important events in the history of the world. If not for this moment, in fact, we wouldn't understand the most beautiful part of the New Testament.

PASSOVER

If you know anything at all about the death of Christ, you'll understand why I get teary when I write this next part. Immediately before the last plague hit, God commanded his people to take a lamb with no blemish, kill it at twilight, and put some of its blood on the doorposts of their homes.

During the night, God said, he would move throughout Egypt, killing every firstborn in the land—"from the firstborn of Pharaoh who sits on the throne, even to the firstborn of the slave girl who is behind the handmill, and all the firstborn of the cattle" (Exod. 11:5). No one would be left out or overlooked. "There shall be a great cry throughout all the land of Egypt, such as there has never been, nor ever will be again" (v. 6).

And then he said this:

> "The blood shall be a sign for you, on the houses where you are. And when I see the blood, I will pass over you, and no plague will befall you to destroy you, when I strike the land of Egypt." (v. 13)

The blood of a perfect lamb, brushed from side to side and top to bottom on a door frame, indicated that those inside were his, rescued by his love for them.

Not these, he whispered. *These are mine.*

And so, when God's wrath swept through Egypt, he did something for his beloved children.

He *passed over* them.

Which is why, to this day, Jewish people celebrate the day that God protected them.

Passover.

The blood sacrifice of an animal, its skin stretched over the fallen man and wife.

The blood of a ram, sent to die in place of the promised child, Isaac.

The unmerited, undeserved, unprecedented favor. The unwavering grace. And, yes, that's the part that should shock us.

"It is impossible for the blood of bulls and goats to take away sins" (Heb. 10:4)—to take them away permanently and completely. Only One could do that, and here in Exodus, we're still hundreds of years away from his first breath.

OVER AND OUT

The final plague hit its mark. A devastated Pharaoh summoned Moses and told him to pack up his crew and leave. In fact, the Egyptians were so eager to get the Israelites out of town that they tossed clothes and jewelry at them as they left. That's next-level in my book.

The Lord had done what he'd promised—had done what he promised Abraham about bringing his people out of their captors' land "with great possessions" (Gen. 15:14)—had done what he promised Moses, how "when you go, you shall not go empty," but would "plunder the Egyptians" in the act of breaking free (Exod. 3:21–22).

Do you remember when Joseph had the happy talk with his family about making sure his bones were brought back to their land? Well, don't worry. Those bones were on board for the trip, rattling around somewhere. (I don't know why I just giggled at this—the fact that it wasn't a short journey, and how it would be a real downer to lose those bones along the way. "WHO'S GOT JOSEPH, Y'ALL?????") But the children of Israel were on their way. Milk and honey, party of thousands. They had a fluffy stack of clouds to guide them during the day and a heavenly fire to guide them at night.

But, as you can probably imagine, things didn't come off without a hitch. (As I write this, we're in the midst of a global pandemic, so it's definitely the season of, "I did NOT see this coming.") Pharaoh changed his mind—sort of a "My bad, I didn't think this all the way through, Moses. I know we've had bloody water and bugs, but we're really going to need y'all to stay here and be our slaves."

So as the Israelites were heading toward their freedom, hundreds of enemy chariots started roaring across the sands toward the slow-moving multitudes. The Egyptians were a whole lot faster in their chariots than the Israelites, what with their screaming babies and bathroom stops. People were yelling at Moses and telling him they'd rather have stayed and been slaves than be killed out here in the middle of nowhere. That feels a little dramatic.

But Moses took it in stride (as much as he could, I'm sure) and called out to God. He'd been given a promise that had been passed down through the generations before him, and I believe he knew somehow, in some way, this was all part of God's mysterious plan.

It's just that the Red Sea and all.

So he spoke over the multitudes, saying:

> "Fear not, stand firm, and see the salvation of the LORD, which he will work for you today. For the Egyptians whom you see today, you shall never see again. The LORD will fight for you, and you have only to be silent." (Exod. 14:13–14)

I've definitely told my kids to be quiet on a road trip, but I don't think those were the words I used. I mean, it probably wouldn't have been the worst thing in the world for the Israelites to just lower their voices. But the point is, they needed to trust that the reason they'd be delivered was because God said so, not because they had the ability to do so on their own.

On God's command, Moses raised his staff in the direction of the Red Sea, and the Lord sent a mighty east wind that blew all night long, parting the waters and simultaneously drying out the riverbed where water had previously been. In addition, the Lord maneuvered the cloud that had stood ahead of the Israelites and repositioned it *behind* them, shrouding the Egyptian warriors in a foggy mist of darkness. God's people were thereby able to hustle safely across between the divided walls of water. Are you thinking what I'm thinking? Killer theme park ride.

Then in the morning, when the Egyptians could see clearly enough to pursue the Hebrews, these same waters broke loose and drowned them *en masse*. They were free from their slave drivers. God had done it.

And if you're still keeping track, that's . . .

Moses: 4

Water: 0

Seems like a good time for a worship service to break out, don't you think?—which is exactly what happened.

> "Sing to the LORD, for he has triumphed gloriously; the horse and his rider he has thrown into the sea." (Exod. 15:21)

But this "Song of Moses," as it's called, takes up only the opening two-thirds of Exodus 15. By the end of that chapter, God's people wouldn't be worshipping anymore. They are legitimately the most fickle group I've ever encountered. They also seem pretty entitled for people who'd just seen God split a sea open for them. I'll add this: I've never seen that particular miracle happen, but I do know I'm not a stranger to being fickle in my relationship with God.

You're going to get to know these folks a little better in the next chapter, but I will warn you—and you'll understand in a few paragraphs . . .

They love their leeks.

Chapter 7

DANCING WITH DISOBEDIENCE
The Wilderness Years

The Israelites were now walking in the direction of the land that would ultimately be theirs. *Finally!* They'd been rescued. Their God had just opened up the sea to save them from being killed. And he'd put these incredible cloud-and-fire navi-thingies in the sky, showing them which way to go. Can't you just hear them praising and cheering and shouting their gratitude into the sky? You'd think, right?

No. They were grumpy. They were hot. They were hungry. They were thirsty. And I bet you can guess who they were mad at. Poor Moses—just a guy who floated in a basket as a kid and took a job he never wanted as a grown-up. Let's give him some grace.

Because do you know how long it had been since they'd walked through water? *Three days.* THREE! And yet . . .

> "Would that we had died by the hand of the LORD in the land of Egypt, when we sat by the meat pots and ate bread to the full, for you have brought us out into this wilderness to kill this whole assembly with hunger." (Exod. 16:3)

Yeah, they told Moses they wanted to go back into slavery, where at least they had leeks and melons. They had onions. They had garlic. And fish. How on earth does freedom hold a candle to some fresh cucumbers?

So, basically, it took them less than half a week to forget their God was all-powerful. Cool. Good job, chosen people. Way to give it the old college try.

But listen: again, it's not like I haven't done the same. I've been given freedom in Christ, and yet I often look back on the things I used to have, and they can seem pretty appealing. But they aren't ultimately good, and I know that. *We know that!*—even though sometimes we wish we could forget the rules and live without any boundaries. That's okay. We're fallen. It's just part of life. But remember this truth when you go through seasons where you're grumbling. *You've been set free.* To go back would be to bind your own wrists and ankles. And trust me, you'd regret it. That's not to say there won't be standards to be upheld for disobedience. But what *are* the rules? Glad you asked.

THE TEN COMMANDMENTS

I didn't mention it when we were there before, but back when God spoke to Moses at the burning bush, he made the following pledge:

> "I will be with you, and this shall be the sign for you, that I have sent you: when you have brought the people out of Egypt, you shall serve God on this mountain." (Exod. 3:12)

And now they were back. Back at the same mountain where the bush had burned. All those months ago, it had been just God and Moses here; now it was God and Moses and (I don't know) maybe a couple of million Israelites. The Lord had led them as promised to the very place where he first appointed Moses as their deliverer. That's some strong proof, I think, of both his power and his faithfulness.

And here on this mountain, God gave to them the ground rules for what he expected of them, written by his own hand on a pair of stone tablets.

Here's the deal. We're going to learn them here, but we can't leave them here. Write them down. A lot of *Christians* don't even know all of them.

So here you go: The Ten Commandments, as given in Exodus 20:

1. "You shall have no other gods before me." (v. 3)
2. "You shall not make for yourself a carved image." (v. 4)
3. "You shall not take the name of the LORD your God in vain." (v. 7)
4. "Remember the Sabbath day, to keep it holy." (v. 8)
5. "Honor your father and your mother." (v. 12)
6. "You shall not murder." (v. 13)
7. "You shall not commit adultery." (v. 14)
8. "You shall not steal." (v. 15)
9. "You shall not bear false witness against your neighbor." (v. 16)
10. "You shall not covet." (v. 17)

Is that all? It's still cool to eat leeks as long as we don't gorge ourselves, right?

But let's be clear about what these commandments are for. They are the standard for how we live obediently as God's people. The first four commandments deal primarily with how we relate to God; the remaining six commandments deal with how we relate to others. That's why when Jesus was asked (we're going to meet him later, and you will LOVE him), "Which is the great commandment?" he answered, "love the Lord your God" and "love your neighbor as yourself" (Matt. 22:36–39). And yet these few commandments—whether ten or just two—are impossible to keep. The standard is too high for us, sinful as we are. We can't do it. We can never be that *good,* not to that level of goodness. Not the way God is good.

So, what's the point? Just hand out a bunch of things we can't obey? And then tell us we have to obey them? That seems a little shady.

But actually, that's the point. *He* is the only One who is good. He doesn't want to see us fail, but we can only succeed if we have his power—because ours is just as useless and fickle as the leek-lovers. We are utterly dependent on him. But don't miss this part: there isn't some heavenly chart that docks us every time we wish we had our friend's house. Or our friend's summer body. (I offer these as hypothetical examples.) He knows we cannot do this without him. But Christ sacrificed himself on our behalf. And in *his* fulfillment of the law—in *our* place—we become free to follow, not forced to follow.

Don't worry if you're still a little confused about where Jesus is in all of this. Just know, even if this is your first exposure to the Bible, you will recognize parts of his life that many seasoned believers have been known to overlook.

Go you.

THE TABERNACLE

Moses couldn't leave these people alone for one hot second before they started acting like idiots again. For example: while he was up there on the mountain getting the tablets of law from the GOD OF THE UNIVERSE, they got restless. One thing led to another (as it always does when your chaperone is otherwise occupied in the clouds), and they decided to melt down all their gold jewelry and stuff, and craft it into the shape of a calf that they could worship instead of God. Can't see how that could go wrong.

This isn't the scene Moses wanted to come back to, obviously. But he eventually got things back under control, and this is where we're introduced to one of the coolest (and most important) objects in Scripture: the *tabernacle*.

I just got choked up. Simply writing the word "tabernacle" is enough to amaze me. But we'll get back to that in a bit. Don't say I didn't warn you.

The tabernacle was a portable sanctuary that Moses told them how to construct according to the exact plans God had given him: "Exactly as I show you concerning the pattern of the tabernacle, and all of its furniture, so you shall make it" (Exod. 25:9).

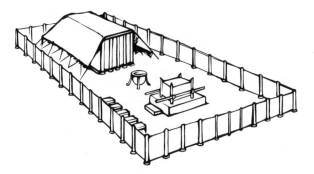

TABERNACLE

Above is a picture of the tabernacle for you, to give you the general idea. You see the fence around it, you see the altar where the priests would make burnt offerings. Then, of course, you see the covered area that included various furnishings that were significant and symbolic in their worship. And all of it was meant to be movable.

Transportable. Everything was capable of being broken down and then set back up as they traveled from place to place. The tabernacle is where God would meet with them. It was representative of his presence among his people, wherever they went. In other words, it is where the spirit of God himself would dwell.

But for the purposes of this book, I want to zero in on one aspect: the ark of the covenant, particularly the "mercy seat" (Exod. 25:17). It's the symbolic area on top of the ark between the sculptured, outstretched wings of two angels. (I've included a second drawing that depicts the ark itself.)

The ark was positioned behind a screen, a veil, in the innermost part of the tabernacle—a key spec that becomes vitally important as the Bible story unfolds. This secluded

ARK OF THE COVENANT

room was known as the "Holy Place" (Lev. 16:2)—more traditionally the *Holy of Holies*. And once a year, on what the Bible calls "the Day of Atonement" (Lev. 23:28), the high priest was to enter this space by himself and appear before the mercy seat, accessing God's forgiveness on behalf of the people.

Have you ever heard of Yom Kippur? Well, now you know what it's referring to. It's the holiest day of the Jewish year. In keeping with custom, they often fast and come together as a group to recite specific prayers. Many of them abstain from work and other ordinary activities. It's a day to reflect on their sins and repent before God so that they will feel forgiven.

As Christians, we may not be as familiar with Yom Kippur because we don't believe God's favor and forgiveness is dependent on our fasting and prayer. Not that those aren't great things; we do both of them as believers. It's just that they're not responsible for maintaining our salvation.

Salvation. This isn't a word you need to be fully familiar with yet. In the New Testament we're going to get a lot more specific. May I also just throw this in? When I was searching the Christian faith and trying to decide if it was something I believed, *salvation* was one of those words I cringed at because it felt so dramatic and heavy-handed. I didn't understand the meaning well enough to let go of my preconceived notions. I do understand it now, but I'm careful about using it in a setting where the context doesn't leave room to clearly explain it.

All I'm saying, in terms of the "Day of Atonement," is that our atonement (another one of those words, I know) has already been bought and paid for. We don't need to keep pleading for it. Jesus, our ultimate high priest, entered "once for all" into the holy place, "not by means of the blood of goats and calves but by means of his own blood, thus securing an eternal redemption" (Heb. 9:12).

Eternal redemption.

Our forgiveness never ends. And nothing we can do will change that.

But the ancient Israelites didn't know this. It wasn't time yet for their Messiah to arrive. And so God provided them with the imagery of the tabernacle to show his desire for meeting with them, for keeping them pure through sacrifice, and for extending his grace to them from his mercy seat. Otherwise, we would be left to ourselves, to the destruction of our frequent disobediences.

Lamb of God, you take away the sins of the world. Have mercy on us.

LEVITICUS

Notice now—from some of the verses I referenced in the previous section—we've inched on into Leviticus, the third book of the Bible. I sometimes refer to Leviticus as "the place where people give up on reading the Bible from Genesis to Revelation." It's mostly just a more detailed version of the laws that God had given, kind of like a guidebook or an owner's manual. It's the information he gave to Moses on the mountain for him to pass along to the people down at sea level.

Think of it this way—all those laws in Leviticus are God's way of fleshing out a fuller version of the Ten Commandments, helping the people understand how to *actually* go about obeying them in their daily lives. As you can imagine, it would get tricky to figure out what each commandment required in the rhythms of everyday life. For instance, what does "keeping the Sabbath day holy" actually mean? *I mean, can we work? Can we eat? Do we do it on the first day of the week or the last? Or on a random Wednesday every other month? And if we can eat, when do we make the food? The day of? Or is that considered work? Maybe the day before? But wait, we don't have refrigerators . . .*

Instead of dropping down the Ten Commandments and saying, "Alrighty! Good luck with that," God offered the levitical laws to fill in the details of what obedience should look like week in and week out. In this way, instead of being burdensome, it actually clarified things.

Let's not forget—these leek-lovers just came out of Egypt, where false gods were considered fickle and capricious. No one knew how to please them. The things that worked one day for the pagan gods didn't work the next. In this way, the law was supposed to be a welcome reprieve— no more guessing or performing and wondering if a deity was pleased. With Yahweh, who is solid and trustworthy and never changes, the people could say, in essence, *This is amazing! We know exactly what to do, and the things God requires of us don't shift from day to day! He won't have a mood swing like other gods. We have the inside track on how to interact with him, and we don't have to wonder if he's pleased or not! Somebody cue the confetti popper!*

There's stuff in there about the various kinds of sacrifices that corresponded to certain seasons or circumstances in people's lives, about making restitution for criminal acts, even for accidents, about what to eat and not eat, about how to treat diseases, about the proper observance of the Sabbath . . .

You get the idea. It's a lot. And from our own historical viewpoint, some of it does seem strangely specific and belaboring, even a little gross in places.

But it establishes holiness and obedience as essential to remaining in proper standing with God, and it introduces the kinds of rules and remedies that made for peaceful, orderly relationship with others in the community.

If you want to hunker down and memorize it, now is your opportunity. I'll be here when you get back.

Anywhooo, the Israelites were traveling with all of this stuff, and they couldn't stop complaining. "Are we almost there yet?" "How much longer, Moses?" "Is there a Chick-fil-A at the next exit?"

Here's the thing: God had shown them he cared about them and their needs; they just weren't great at remembering it. They once griped about the drinking water being bitter at one of the first places they stopped, and the Lord told Moses to throw a log into it. (Don't ask. I have no idea why.) The water instantly became sweet. After another of their complaining episodes, God arranged for massive quantities of quail to blow in from the sea and hover two feet off the ground. I think we can all agree this was a miracle, but I don't know how I feel about hovering ocean quails. Also, he started regularly giving the people a yummy, original brand of food called *manna* that miraculously appeared on the ground each morning, ready for gathering. One of the psalm writers called it "the bread of the angels" (Ps. 78:25)—that's how tasty it was.

But around the time when they were hankering for their old Egyptian leeks and garlic, the Bible reports them saying something about how "our strength is dried up, and there is nothing at all but this manna to look at" (Num. 11:6). Apparently, the angel food cake wasn't good enough for them, and as expected, they went back to the leeks thing. They sound awesome.

All this to say, they finally ended up at the border of Canaan—the dream land they'd been picturing in their mind's eye ever since Moses had first described it, way back in the slave pits of Egypt. The only thing God commanded them to do before they entered in and began occupying it was to send twelve men—one from each of the twelve tribes of Israel (hey-oooooh!)—to spy out the land and bring back a report on its inhabitants, its layout, and its general condition.

No problem. These twelve fellas set out on their mission, which took them a total of forty days. (Remember what I told you about the number forty in the Bible? A period of testing?) And upon their return, they confirmed everything Moses had said about what this Promised Land was like. Truly, they said, "it flows with milk and honey" (Num. 13:27). They even brought back big clusters of fruit that they'd stolen. Evidently, the commandment on stealing had fallen apart pretty quickly. I mean, they'd made it clear that food was a priority to them, and as an Italian woman, I can totally get down with that.

Kiss the manna goodbye, friends. We've finally hit the jackpot. And did anyone say thank you to Moses? Apologize for their behavior? Doubt it.

But the spies weren't done telling the rest of their neighbors what they'd seen. Everything was exactly the way it was supposed to be in Canaan, except for this one little detail about the people who already lived there—people so big that they made our guys look like grasshoppers. They'd never be able to win a fight against them. The cities were well protected, and again—there were *giants*! So, looks like this whole thing might have been a misunderstanding.

Except that two of the spies, Joshua and Caleb, were confident they could do it. They believed in God's promises and were ready to take him up on them. They tried to convince everyone that this is exactly where they were supposed to be, and God would never have led them all the way here just to lose a battle he told them they would win. *Look at everything he's done so far!* they were saying. *This is part of the promise!!!*

So, "let us go up at once and occupy it," said Caleb, "for we are well able to overcome it" (Num. 13:30). Yes, added Joshua, "Do not rebel against the Lord. And do not fear the people of the land, for they are bread for us. Their protection is removed from them, and the Lord is with us; do not fear them" (Num. 14:9).

That was very moving, boys. But the anthem-like, end-of-the-movie song was not actually playing where everyone else could hear it, and the people said they needed to calm down with all this nonsense. They weren't Rudy on a football field. They were whiners who were going to die.

This was not what God wanted. So he stepped into the conversation with a couple of STRONG THOUGHTS for Moses:

"How long shall this wicked congregation grumble against me? . . . Say to them, 'As I live, declares the LORD, what you have said in my hearing I will do to you: your dead bodies shall fall in this wilderness, and all of your number, listed in the census from twenty years old and upward, who have grumbled against me, not one of them shall come into the land where I swore that I would make you dwell.'" (vv. 27–30)

All but two: Caleb and Joshua.

The rest of them—all two million minus two of them— would, instead, wander the wilderness until each one of them dropped dead in their tracks. In other words, there'd be a lot more bones than just Joseph's. And this journey would last a full year for each day, all *forty* days, that the faithless spies had spent investigating the land. The blessing of their inheritance would revert instead to their children. Their kids and grandkids would inherit the land that their ancestors rejected. But to this "wicked congregation who are gathered together against me: in this wilderness they shall come to a full end, and there they shall die" (v. 35).

Just like Adam and Eve way back when, even with paradise right in front of them, they didn't believe God. Again and again and again, after God had split seas and rained down bread from the sky and even given them *ocean quail*, they refused to believe him. And it's not like he hadn't given them a chance. But just like Adam and Eve, the consequence for unbelief and rebellion was death.

Listen, we are all a mess when it comes to consistency with trusting God. And while it's normal to have those thoughts, it isn't appropriate to follow up by being rebellious. There are definitely consequences for our disobedience. That's not just true in the *Old* Testament; it's true in the New Testament and in our lives as well.

As Hebrews 3 says, this time echoing Psalm 95:

> Today, if you hear his voice, do not harden your hearts as in the rebellion, on the day of testing in the wilderness, where your fathers put me to the test and saw my works for forty years. Therefore I was provoked with that generation, and said, "They will always go astray in their heart; they have not known my ways." As I swore in my wrath, "They shall not enter my rest." (Heb. 3:7–11)

Lord Jesus, help us believe that all we need to do is stand still, obey, and honor you in the process. How often we forget that he's already gone before us. Through water and desert, through hospital and school, through home and highway. I pray I don't miss the gifts he's wanted me to have because I refused to trust the hand that offered it.

NUMBERS

Again, as with Leviticus, did you see how I slipped us into the book of Numbers without even telling you? Numbers starts out kind of slow, with lots of census figures and such. It's sort of like reading the *World Almanac*. It's definitely not the mental break you feel you deserve after the whole Leviticus thing. But soon enough, it opens up into a collection of stories (like the one about the twelve spies) that chronicles this forty years of wandering.

That's what Numbers is. ARE YOU READY FOR THIS? It's the story of the Israelites wandering in the wilderness— their grumbling, their sin, their rebellion, and lots of other nice, happy thoughts like that. So whenever somebody says, in referring to a particular Bible story or passage, "Hey, isn't that in the book of Numbers?" you can now access the part of your brain that says, "Numbers records the time period after the Exodus, before the Israelites had entered the Promised Land."

Boom. Done.

See? It's not so bad.

DEUTERONOMY

While we're at it, what do you say we go ahead and solve the mystery of Deuteronomy too? The forty years of wandering had elapsed by now. The whole generation of grumblers had died out, and it was time for round two. Moses had led the people round and round in circles, and finally he'd maneuvered them back to the borders of Canaan again.

Let's hope it goes a lot better this time than last.

The big news, really, is that while Joshua and Caleb and this new crop of Israelites were all set to lay claim to the land that their parents and grandparents had literally been *dying* for them to see, God declared that Moses, um . . .

Well, this is going to be the time for us to hug him and wish him well, because he isn't going with them.

And wait until you hear why. If I could, I'd change this part of the Bible.

He had gotten frustrated with the Israelites, which we can completely understand. And after listening to God's instructions for how to deal with them, Moses struck a rock twice with his shepherd's staff instead of speaking to it. And this seemingly slight act of self-will and rebellion is what would keep him out of the Promised Land.

That feels pretty intense, given the level of infraction compared to the amount of time and hassle the guy had gone through. He obeyed God so many times in the previous decades, and this one incident is all it takes to keep him out?

Yeah, looks that way.

God had called him from a nice, settled life to one of the hardest jobs anyone's ever been tasked with undertaking. And yet he'd stood tall against Pharaoh. He'd raised his arms in faith over the Red Sea. He'd put up with the people's complaining and had persevered faithfully in the wilderness. Back when they'd been ready to stone Caleb and Joshua, and the Lord had said to him, "I will strike them with the pestilence and disinherit them, and I will make of you a nation greater and mightier than they" (Num. 14:12), Moses pleaded with God not to do it. He knew the Lord to be "slow to anger and abounding in steadfast love, forgiving iniquity and transgression" (v. 18).

Clever. I should've tried that with my parents.

I've wondered if it had something to do with the fact that God had called him to this task while he was hiding from the Egyptians as a shepherd. I don't know for sure. In any case, it's time for him to extinguish his torch and leave the island.

Still, I love this next part. It's where I decided I loved Moses. Don't be intimidated by the name of the book—Deuteronomy—because (surprise) you already have the exact tools you need to understand it. Ready? It is simply the last five speeches Moses gave to the Israelites to remind them of where they'd come from and where they were called to be. It is an encouragement, an assignment, a reminder, and a love letter—a reminder that they were his chosen people, and they should go in there like they believe it. Just think: not all of them knew the full history. Their parents did, but now there's a whole new crew that needs to be reminded of heritage and hope.

Moses was so incredible. And his speeches are so strong and full of fatherly wisdom. The best part is that I promise you if you decide to skip over there sometime and read a little bit, you'll be encouraged. Hear a few of his words:

> "You have stayed long enough at this mountain. Turn and take your journey. . . . Go in and take possession of the land that the LORD swore to your fathers, to Abraham, to Isaac, and to Jacob, to give to them and to their offspring after them." (Deut. 1:6–8)

Don't you feel like clapping along too?—not just for what these people are about to experience, but because you're feeling the power of actually understanding the story of the Bible? It is so, so beautiful.

I can just picture Moses there. The Bible says despite his age (120 years) and all the stress he'd been through, "his eye was undimmed, and his vigor unabated" (Deut. 34:7). It's not as though he was too old and crotchety to keep going. God had been faithful to him, and faithful to his people too. Moses reminded them how, although they'd been constantly on the move for these forty long years, "your clothes have not worn out on you, and your sandals have not worn off your feet" (Deut. 29:5).

He wasn't unclear with them about the way they should proceed. He highlighted the promises, as well as the punishments. They could choose which they wanted to prioritize.

> "I have set before you today life and good, death and evil. If you obey the commandments of the LORD your God that I command you today, by loving the LORD your God, by walking in his ways, and by keeping his commandments and his statutes and his rules, then you shall live and multiply, and the LORD your God will bless you in the land

that you are entering to take possession of it." (Deut. 30:15–16)

But . . .

"If your heart turns away, and you will not hear, but are drawn away to worship other gods and serve them, I declare to you today, that you shall surely perish. You shall not live long in the land that you are going over Jordan to enter and possess." (vv. 17–18)

Here, then, was the plain and simple of it:

"I have set before you life and death, blessing and curse. Therefore choose life, that you and your offspring may live, loving the LORD your God, obeying his voice and holding fast to him, for he is your life and length of days." (vv. 19–20)

And so ends the saga of this first, five-book section of the Bible.

Except for this touching farewell. And you might want to grab a tissue. Unless you're dead inside.

God took Moses high up on a mountain—just the two of them—so that Moses could gaze down from above and see with his own eyes the land he'd been forbidden from entering. And there, God gently and graciously buried him. Yes, *God himself* took total care of Moses' funeral arrangements. And to this day, the Bible says, no one knows the place where he laid his faithful servant to rest. The tender care of our Father in this moment just absolutely slays me.

I told you I've struggled with God's decision to draw Moses up short of the Promised Land, which *no one* seemed more deserving of being the first to set foot into.

In my perfect-ending scenario, this story would've looked a lot different.

But here's the part that makes me weepy. Moments after Moses was blocked from going into Canaan, God brought him immediately into his presence, into eternal life. Moses' loss in the grand picture of things was only temporary. It paled in comparison to what was coming up next for him.

And I hope, in hearing me say this, it brings you the peace you may be desperately needing right now . . . because the God who carried Moses to eternity will do the same for you as a believer in Christ. The disappointments that may be strangling you today will soon be forgotten, completely overshadowed by the glories of his presence that await you. And even though his hands may not dig the physical dirt that lays you to rest, they will surely carry you to heaven. You'll be raised from this old, busted earth and resurrected by hand into a *new* earth.

Who can understand a love like this? Not me.

But have courage, friend.

He has gone before you.

Chapter 8

CANAAN, HERE WE COME
Conquest and Consequences

 I'm reflecting back on that part of the story we covered many, many pages ago: "So Abram went, as the Lord had told him . . . and they set out to go to the land of Canaan" (Gen. 12:4–5). Don't look now but—*here they are!*—this enormous nation of people who, at that moment when "Abram went," were not even a twinkle in their father's eye.

This is just so epically incredible, I don't even know how to say it.

And yet the woven thread keeps extending forward to the next edition of Israel's people. Moses, near the end of Deuteronomy, had summoned Joshua and commissioned him as their new leader. Good choice. He will prove to be brave, daring, and faithful, different in style but no less amazing than the great leader who came before him.

So at the beginning of the book that bears Joshua's name—which, remember, is the first of twelve that comprise the historical books of the Old Testament—the Lord appeared to him with the promise that, "just as I was with Moses, so I will be with you. I will not leave you or forsake you" (Josh. 1:5). *Be strong and courageous.* Those are the words God repeatedly shares with this new commander of the Israelite people.

And now we come to one of my favorite stories from Scripture. (I know, I have a lot of favorite stories. You've probably noticed.) The story I'm talking about here is the story of *Rahab*. And kind of like how I told you I feel about Jacob, I have thanked God many times for choosing someone like Rahab to include as a player in his story.

But before I describe her any further for you, allow me a brief yet somewhat related diversion. Do you remember my telling you how one of the things that makes the Bible tricky to understand is that the books don't always appear in strict, chronological order? The book of *Ruth* is an example of that. I know we're skipping ahead a couple of books to reach the place where it's located—between Judges and 1 Samuel—but Ruth is a stand-alone story that's mainly important for a couple of reasons.

1. *Ruth ended up playing a featured role in Israel's history, even though she herself was not born an Israelite.* She married a young Jewish man whose family had migrated to her home country of Moab from Bethlehem during a season of famine. But the man died, leaving her to widowhood. And when her mother-in-law, Naomi—who'd also been widowed—returned home years later, Ruth demanded to go along with her: "Where you go I will go, and where you lodge I will lodge. Your people shall be my people, and your God my God" (Ruth 1:16). Name five women you know who would beg their mothers-in-law to bring them along for years of quality time. Yeah. Ruth was quite a selfless gal. Because, let me tell you, Naomi was a piece of work. She was bitter and a less-than-ideal travel partner.

2. *Ruth's life was forever changed by a man who served as her redeemer.* Back in Bethlehem, Ruth caught the eye of a wealthy landowner named Boaz, who in the social structure of that day was considered a "redeemer" in relation to Naomi's family (Ruth 2:20)—meaning, as a close kin, he was one of the men who was chiefly responsible for taking care of anything she or her household might need. In this

way, Boaz is a foreshadowing of Christ—someone related to us who becomes our needed Redeemer.

You can probably see where this is going. Boaz married Ruth. Though a Jewish man, he *redeemed* her—a person whom no one would ever have expected to be included in God's covenant—a non-Jew, also referred to as a Gentile.

But the real kicker to Ruth's story comes at the tail end of the book, where the Bible says Ruth had a child named Obed, who would grow up to have a child named Jesse, who would grow up to have a child named David, who would grow up into adulthood to become King David, whose family tree would include a child by the name of Jesus.

So the next time you're reading at the beginning of the New Testament, where Matthew begins his Gospel with a listing of the "genealogy of Jesus Christ" (Matt. 1:1), look to see if you don't find Ruth's name appearing there as sort of an unexpected member of Jesus' lineage. Isn't that cool, how God deliberately wove an outsider into such a significant chain of pedigree?

But right there next to Ruth's name in Matthew 1 is the name of another unlikely Old Testament character. Because by another astounding example of God's providence, Ruth's husband Boaz—the great-grandfather of King David, remember—was the son of a woman named Rahab.

Let's get back to the prostitute. Oh, wait—maybe I didn't mention that Rahab was a lady of the evening, but she was.

First, let's remember where we are. The Israelites had wandered around for forty years as punishment for their doubt, and the next generation showed back up on the doorstep of Canaan to hang with the grasshoppers. Joshua sent a couple of fresh spies into the land, hoping it would go better than the first time around, and they ended up at Rahab's house (it's not for the reason you might guess, btw, thank goodness), which was built into the wall that surrounded the city. Scripture says they were about to invade Jericho, but didn't we just read that they were going into Canaan? It's okay. Jericho was simply one of the border cities in the region of Canaan.

ABRAHAM TO DAVID TO JESUS

Now when the spies had entered Canaan the first time, forty years earlier, they just naturally assumed the native people of the land would take one look at these spindly Israelites and think they could eat them for breakfast. That's how insecurity generally works. We write the script of what other people are thinking, and then we build our responses around it.

From what Rahab said, though, the spies learned that their predecessors' hunches had been dead wrong. The Canaanites were in fact *terrified* of them. "All the inhabitants of the land melt away before you," she said (Josh. 2:9). They'd heard what God had done for them, as far back as the Red Sea crossing and the horrible plagues and all that, and they knew the manufactured gods and idols of Canaan wouldn't stand a chance against this Yahweh they'd been told about.

The spies, of course, couldn't wait to get back to their countrymen to tell them the news, to see their eyes light up at the sound of this fresh intel. But Jericho was still a dangerous place. And getting these two guys out of there safely was no small task. Rahab, though, was the kind of girl who could do it. Based on her, ahem, professional experience, she was among the best at knowing how to keep men's secrets. By employing a method that had probably proven successful in the past, she hid them on her rooftop under stalks of flax. And when some folks came to her door asking if she had seen them, she lied. She kept them hidden there until night fell, but she had one request before she helped them escape by way of a rope from her window. She asked to be spared, along with her family, when Israel did come to attack Jericho. They agreed, telling her that in order for the Hebrew soldiers to know which house to spare, she would need to mark it by letting down a crimson cord.

The sight of scarlet—like the red of the Passover blood, like the red of our Savior's blood—would mark her house as one where guilty sinners could go to be saved.

Sinners like Rahab.

Sinners like us.

So the guys got out and passed along their experiences. The Israelites were fired up to move in now. Only one problem: they found themselves on the wrong side again of another impassable expanse of water. The Jordan River had become their new Red Sea.

And here's what I'd like to say about that. When Israel had gotten this close to the Promised Land a generation before, they were positioned to the south. In the desert. All they'd needed to do was just walk in, all two million of them. Footprints in the sand. But now, forty years later, they were all the way around to the east, where entry into Canaan required crossing the Jordan at flood stage. WE ARE NOT AFRAID OF THE MAPS.

God appears to have a thing for making water stop, because in Joshua 3, he did it again. Per God's instructions, the priests lined up at the head of the crowd, carrying the ark of the covenant. And as soon as their feet touched water, God miraculously caused the Jordan to dam up, well north of their location, allowing the entire nation to walk through on dry ground.

Again, amazing. Rank by rank they proceeded to the other side, where Joshua did something really significant—something we'd all do well to learn from and apply at special moments in our lives today. After everyone had made it across, he ordered twelve men—one from each tribe—to walk back into the dry riverbed, select a sizable rock, hoist it onto one shoulder, then carry it to the Canaan side of the Jordan. These stones would be a visible sign—a "memorial," he said—for future generations. It would help them remember what God had done for them on this incredible day.

> "When your children ask in time to come, 'What do those stones mean to you?' then you shall tell them that the waters of the

Jordan were cut off before the ark of the
covenant of the LORD. . . . These stones shall
be to the people of Israel a memorial forever." (Josh. 4:6–7)

"A memorial forever." *Let's not forget God's faithfulness,*
Joshua was telling them. *Let's leave our kids a physical
reminder that says God met us here at an impossible place,
and he didn't let us down.*

But I can't leave you here without sewing a bit more
of this together, because it's often the details that make a
story beautiful.

Rahab and her family were safe and sound after the
invasion of the Israelites, which is a good thing because if
she hadn't survived, you never would have met her son a
few paragraphs ago.

Boaz.

Kinsman redeemer and foreshadowing of Christ. Born
to the most unlikely mother and rescued by a blood-red
cord dropped into the dark under a sky full of stars too
numerous to count.

FROM JERICHO FORWARD

The book of Joshua can be summarized as the account
of Israel's exploits as they entered Canaan. It takes them
across the Jordan River and tells how they slowly took possession of their Promised Land through battle.

Because life, you know—that's just what it is, a lot of
the time. It's a battle. God makes all our provision for us,
of course, but it's still not an easy process. Just because
the way forward may be a real struggle for you doesn't
mean you're out of God's will. The name *Israel,* remember, includes this whole idea of "striving"—striving against
God; God's striving with us. Even his plans of victory for
us are most often plans for hard-fought battle.

But then sometimes there's Jericho—where God just says, *Watch THIS.*

Remember that old spiritual about Joshua fighting the battle of Jericho? Well, this is the Joshua, and this is the Jericho. And don't be surprised if "the walls come a-tumbling down."

Because that's exactly what happened. Joshua instructed his troops to march silently around the city, once a day for six days, along with seven priests (from the tribe of . . . YES YOU DID) carrying ram's horns, walking along with the ark of the covenant.

Finally on the seventh day, God's orders said to march around the city *seven* times (the number seven in the Bible is associated with perfection or completion), while the priests at the head of the ark blasted away on their trumpets. Then at the end of their last circuit, the people were to let out a primal war cry. The walls, God said, would crumble at the sound.

Sounds like a killer military strategy.

But here's what I know for sure: Joshua had seen Israel at their most disobedient. He'd seen what going against God's commands had cost them. So no matter how crazy this seven-day march thing sounded to his military instincts, Joshua knew obeying God's orders was the right thing to do. *Guys, we're going to believe God this time and do exactly what he says and how he says it. Boots on. Trumpets up. Let us not forget his faithfulness.*

The walls, of course, fell down just as God said they would. The Israelites rushed into the city and burned it to the ground. They then marched onward from there into the rest of the Promised Land, choosing always to obey the Lord, to faithfully trust his word, and to keep his commands top-of-mind for the rest of their lives.

The End.

HAHAHAHAHAHA. *Lies!*

The new-and-improved Israelites turned out to be just as fickle and forgetful as the old dead ones. And yet God continued to lead them deeper into Canaan's interior, until by the end of the book of Joshua they'd pretty much gotten the whole region under their control.

I'm skipping over some great stories you'll want to go back and read for yourself someday. But around the middle part of the book of Joshua, the people divvied up the property, allotting a particular portion of Canaan to each Hebrew tribe. (Though not for the Levites, remember.) (Oh, and not to the descendants of Joseph either, but rather to two of his sons. Why do I even need to remind you? You can teach this by now.)

And that's how the book draws to a close. In relative calm. "The LORD had given rest to Israel from all their surrounding enemies" (Josh. 23:1). Joshua was now an old man—"well advanced in

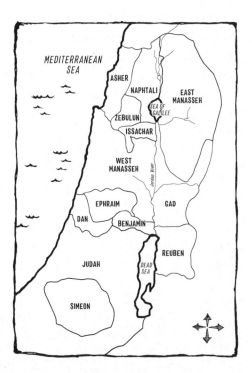

THE TRIBES OF ISRAEL

years," and in his last recorded act" he summoned the people together and walked them through a highlight reel of their history as a nation—a history that you, too, are now personally a part of, and personally familiar with.

Let's just hope the now-established people of Israel had learned something too. They were certainly *saying* the right things: "The LORD our God we will serve, and his voice we will obey" (Josh 24:24). But would it hold?

Mere words rarely do.

But at least the next time you see the carved wooden sign that says, "As for me and my household we will serve the Lord," you'll know where it came from.

That way, when you hang it up, you'll remember that the goal is to do a better job than the ones who originally whittled it into existence.

THE JUDGES

Seems like I remember Moses saying, a long time ago:

> "When the LORD your God brings you into the land that you are entering to take possession of it, and clears away many nations before you . . . and when the LORD your God gives them over to you, and you defeat them, then you must devote them to complete destruction." (Deut. 7:1–2)

Wipe. Them. Out.

I get how, at face value, this kind of take-no-prisoners mandate from God makes him out to be a cruel killer of men, women, and children. But here's what God knew that we need to know, and certainly what the Israelites needed to know. Playing nice with the people they encountered in Canaan could only end badly.

These weren't populations whose customs were just misunderstood. These were people who participated in acts of bestiality and child sacrifice. These were people who possessed no internal restrictions on their wanton, debased idolatry. The Lord knew that interacting and intermarrying with the Canaanite demographic would make compromise a way of life for the Israelites. It would be like, *Join us on the mountain at 6:00 for refreshments and Baal worship. Bring your own god if you want, and your kids to toss onto the sacrifice, and we'll all have a big party together.* That's the only way things were going to turn out for Israel unless the entire land was cleansed of this element.

But they were only willing to take God's commandments so far. They were not willing to stop dancing with disobedience whenever it suited them or when it felt like the better alternative. Instead they started to make friends with these people, to cozy up to the parts of their daily lives that they found most attractive, to assimilate into their cultures rather than realize God's commands were intended for his people's protection. And just as Moses had predicted back in Deuteronomy 7 and elsewhere—when he told them to go into Canaan and "break down their altars" and "dash in pieces their pillars" and "chop down" their sacred idols and "burn their carved images with fire" (v. 5)—the people's half-hearted obedience came back to bite them.

Here, then, is the state of affairs at the beginning of the book of Judges:

> The people of Israel did what was evil in the sight of the LORD and served the Baals. And they abandoned the LORD, the God of their fathers, who had brought them out of the land of Egypt. They went after other gods, from among the gods of the people who were around them, and bowed down to them. (Judg. 2:11–12)

Therefore . . .

> The anger of the LORD was kindled against
> Israel, and he gave them over to plunderers,
> who plundered them. And he sold them into
> the hand of their surrounding enemies, so
> that they could no longer withstand their
> enemies. (v. 14)

Yes, they'd been warned about this—*like, 74,736 times!*
So although they could've been enjoying the peace and
prosperity that God had promised them—though they
could've been relishing the blessed satisfaction of finally
being settled in a land they could call their own—their condition instead could be capsuled in the following statement:

> And they were in terrible distress. (v. 15)

I think we can all relate to that.

But God, their covenant pursuer, even as he allowed
them to learn their loyalty lessons the hard way, continued
moving toward them with help and rescue.

So now we're going to meet the judges. They were a com-
bination of military deliverer and civil ruler. There are at
least twelve of them in the book. And throughout this period
of Israel's history, which covered approximately three hundred years, God raised up a revolving door of them.

Think of the book of Judges as a repeating, four-part
cycle, recurring over and over.

1. The people would act right for a while.
2. Then they would fall again into sin and
   rebellion.
3. Sin invited punishment, usually from
   foreign oppressors.
4. The people would then cry out to God
   for mercy.

Tell me if this cycle feels personal to you, as personal as it feels to me. Have you ever struggled with an area of sin in your life, enough until you found yourself suffering your own hard consequences from it? From down there in that pit of guilt, shame, and painfulness, you made all kinds of promises to God about how you'd never do this again. And you meant it, you really did. You didn't ever want to do again the things you'd done that had put you there. But as time went by, the pit lost some of its tangible horror. You started to grow lackadaisical, not guarding yourself quite as carefully. And so, despite the promises you'd made in your season of desperation, you ended up returning to that same awful spot. What happened then? You cried out to God; you repented of what you'd done; you promised you'd do better—if only he would come and get you out of it, one more time.

That's what was happening on a grand scale during the book of Judges. And each time at the bottom of that circle, God would elevate another person to spearhead battles on the people's behalf, leading them out of oppression.

These skirmishes they led against enemy tribes took place at nearly every point on the Canaanite compass. It was Israel continually needing to fight those nations that they'd failed to thoroughly annihilate when they had the chance, the way God had told them.

Most of the judges are not well-known to us. There are a couple of them whose names you might have heard, though perhaps you didn't know they were judges. Gideon, for example—the timid man who God commanded to whittle down his army from thirty thousand to three hundred. Deborah, a woman so courageously wise that not even the bravest soldiers of her day would dare go into battle without her counsel and support. And maybe Samson, with the long hair and massive strength. Delilah really did a number on him, I'll tell you that. He lost his hair and his power, but sometimes that's what happens when you like the way someone looks and you decide to crawl in a tent together. You swipe right and say goodbye to everything you've got.

But even some of the less familiar judges can be quite entertaining to read about. If you've felt as though some of the recent books we've studied have been a little on the boring side—Leviticus, Numbers, Deuteronomy, etc.—Judges is definitely going to give us some serious action. There are knives in the stomach; tent pegs through the head; jars crashing by torchlight, scaring their enemies to death. What would the story be without foxes tied together by the tails, set on fire and turned loose in the grain fields?

Did you know that setting fires and torturing animals are two of the major indicators that a child could grow up to be a serial killer? This is somewhat unrelated but still useful to keep in your back pocket in case your neighbor microwaves his cat.

Judges is a wild ride, and it stays that way until Samuel comes along. Not that it's going to be perfect, but at least a step in the right direction.

Right after the book of Ruth comes the first book of two that are named "Samuel." Ironically, the first one is called 1 Samuel.

Let's get to it. This guy is fascinating. He's got a wacky aunt, if that's what you call your dad's other wife in a polygamous relationship. (So complicated.) And his mom may or may not have been hammered in a temple.

SAMUEL

Before we get to Samuel, let's meet his mom, Hannah. She was infertile, and to make matters worse, her husband's other wife was, umm . . . not.

It was a rotten situation obviously, made worse by the fact that this rival wife within her own home "used to provoke her grievously to irritate her" (1 Sam. 1:6). I've wondered at times if Hannah ever got to the end of her rope and shouted back, "Yeah, well, maybe I don't have a baby yet, Peninnah, but—your name is still Peninnah!" Just a thought I've had.

Anyway, the whole bunch of them were in the habit of traveling each year to Shiloh, a centrally located city which had become the religious hub of Israel, home to the now semipermanent tabernacle, known by this time as the "house of the Lord." And on one particular year's pilgrimage, Hannah drifted over near the tabernacle area by herself. Apparently, she was overcome with her emotions and ended up weeping inconsolably and whispering under her breath, which made the priest assume she was drunk. He confronted her about it, but she explained that she was, in fact, sober.

I want to note something here because I think it's interesting. Although Eli the priest could see her mouth moving, we have no reason to believe he knew what she was saying. So he wouldn't necessarily know she was praying for a son, and he likely didn't know she made a vow to God that if he would give her a little boy, she would "give him to the Lord all the days of his life" (v. 11).

He blessed her and told her to go in peace, asking the Lord to grant her petition.

Sometime later, Hannah did give birth to a son, Samuel, and true to her word, she brought him to the temple as soon as he was weaned. On that yearly day of sacrifice, she offered her son to Eli. She wanted to keep her promise to God. She explained all of this to Eli and told him that Samuel should be raised there in service to the Lord, then she worshipped God in prayer, leaving her son behind as she traveled home. Part of her prayer includes a verse you may have seen before, and I wonder if the context will surprise you:

"For this child I prayed, and the LORD has granted me my petition that I made to him. Therefore I have lent him to the LORD. As long as he lives, he is lent to the LORD." (vv. 27–28)

Usually when it's done in calligraphy over a baby's bed, it stops before it gets to the "and now I'm going to give him away" part.

Now here's what I'm wondering: What if Eli never heard her make that promise? I mean, she could have just enrolled Samuel in some spiritual classes in Shiloh and acted like it never happened. Who knows?

And this leads me to a point I'll be making regularly as we go. There are stories you have heard and paintings you have seen that are completely inaccurate (or at least misleading) based on what the Bible actually says. Remember back in Genesis? Well, we don't know if Eve actually ate an apple or if it was just some other kind of fruit (which is more likely). Jonah was swallowed by a sea creature, but it wasn't necessarily a whale. This is going to get a whole lot more intense when we get into the New Testament, and I can pretty much guarantee you that you'll be shocked at some of the things I tell you.

Never read the Bible without a curious spirit. Dig into the words and see if you notice details that you may not have seen before. For example, we're told that every year Hannah made her son a little robe. Did she hand it to him? Did she ever see him again after she left him in the temple? I hope so, but Scripture never explicitly says that. It's so easy to make leaps and assumptions about the subtext when, in fact, the Bible doesn't specify. Again, this is going to be key when we get to the life of Christ.

Turns out Eli, however, despite being a respected priest, was never nominated for parent of the year, raising boys who were described as "worthless men" who "did not know the LORD" (1 Sam. 2:12). He allowed them to go around masquerading as priests before the people, despite their practice of gorging their own appetites on meat from the burnt offerings and sleeping with the women who served at the tabernacle. So, essentially, Eli the priest was raising someone else's kid (Samuel) and two frat boys.

You can bet God wasn't about to just let this situation slide. In fact, he had some bad news coming to these two young men, as well as to Eli for not doing much to make them shape up. Thankfully, Samuel was a good kid, and the Lord chose him to become the prophetic bridge between the age of the judges and a new day in Israel's history.

Context, context, context! If you've been around church to any extent, even if only as a child, you've probably heard the line from Scripture that says, "Speak, LORD, for your servant is listening." Well, here's the place where it comes from, right here in this story. Samuel was asleep in his little bed one night when he heard a voice calling his name. Hopping up, he wandered into Eli's room. "Here I am!" *You called, sir?*

"I did not call; lie down again," Eli said (1 Sam. 3:5).

Um, okay . . . night, then.

This same thing happened a couple more times until Eli realized, oh—this was *God* calling out to Samuel. "Go, lie down," the old man said to the boy at last. "And if he calls you, you shall say, 'Speak, LORD, for your servant hears'" (v. 9). He did. And Samuel listened. God told him that the sins of Eli's sons were soon to come crashing down on their heads, which Eli (when Samuel shared it with him) was perceptive enough to realize as being fair punishment. Good news and bad news always seemed to commingle with these folks.

So as Samuel continued to grow and more regularly hear from God in Shiloh, it became clear that time was ticking on the status quo. The Philistines, a hostile group of neighboring people who would become one of their most frequent, notorious enemies, showed up and killed four thousand Israelite soldiers in a single battle. Shaken, the surviving troops called for Eli's sons to hustle over from Shiloh with the ark of the covenant, the symbol of God's presence. But the Philistines, recognizing the Israelites were rallying, fought even harder, killing *thirty* thousand men and capturing the ark of the covenant besides.

Eli's two frat boys—ahem, sons—Hophni and Phineas, died in the crossfire. BYYEEEEEEE.

And Eli, sitting at home, hearing the news about the ark being taken, fell backward off his chair and broke his neck. BYYEEEEEEE.

(And now we can never say God doesn't care about hypocritical, negligent, immoral religious leaders.)

So the leadership space in Israel was open again.

And Samuel was the man to fill it.

All throughout his life, he traveled in a circuit from one town to the next, representing God's counsel and guidance to the entire nation. Much as Moses and Joshua had done in years past, he urged the people to "put away the foreign gods and the Ashtaroth from among you and direct your heart to the LORD and serve him only" (1 Sam. 7:3). I think we've all danced with danger with the Ashtaroth, am I right?

So the Philistines had the ark of the covenant, but its arrival coincided with a nationwide outbreak of a massive, mysterious disease. (Ever seen one of those?) Somebody finally connected the dots, chalked it up as being a curse from Israel's God, and decided to send the ark back where it came from. BYYEEEEEEE. This put it safely back in the possession of its rightful owners, which Samuel interpreted as a second chance—*if* everybody would get the message and get on the same page with God again.

I'll give you one guess what happened next. New day, same old sins.

I have no clue what that must be like. (Ahem.)

Onward, folks. Eventually we're going to get away from all of this cycle stuff. You know, like, when we get to glory.

Chapter 9

HOW THE MIGHTY HAVE FALLEN
Kingdom and Collapse

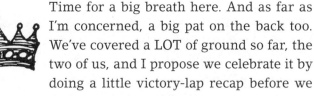

Time for a big breath here. And as far as I'm concerned, a big pat on the back too. We've covered a LOT of ground so far, the two of us, and I propose we celebrate it by doing a little victory-lap recap before we launch into a major new section of Scripture.

Just for fun, go back to page 14 and trace your finger along the thread that runs from Creation to the Exodus, then on throughout the twists and turns of the Wandering years, the entrance of the people into their Promised Land, then all the way up to the time of the Judges. In case you hadn't been counting, the length of road you just walked is equal to roughly 240 chapters of Old Testament Bible. You've been through eight whole books. And now you have the gist of all that material, of all those years, firmly embedded into your biblical brain.

I AM THE PROUDEST TEACHER ON THE FACE OF THE EARTH.

We've covered the judges (the last one was Samuel), and now we're jumping back into Scripture, in the book of 1 Samuel, where we find him getting older and a new leader needing to be chosen.

The Israelites had a plan for that.

"Appoint for us a king to judge us like all the nations." (1 Sam. 8:5)

All the cool kids have kings, Sam. And do we? NO. No, we don't.

In their minds, the fact that they still appeared to be twelve separate tribes was a disadvantage, and the only way to make them look more powerful and consolidated was to have a king. *A disjointed group of smaller tribes that can't compete for top spot in the world's eyes? Nah. Let's be a big, fat kingdom like the hotshot nations around us.*

Samuel knew it was a mistake. God told him so, and he passed along the message to everyone. But, unfortunately, they weren't negotiating, so the search for a king began.

Be careful what you wish for. You might just get it.

SAUL

From the way things started, it looked like this whole business of having a king over Israel might just turn out pretty handsomely after all. Their first king, Saul, seemed to be exactly what they had hoped for. He was tall. Manly. Admirable. Surely this would be the guy to make them known throughout the world as a force. A powerful nation led by a mighty king.

Saul's victories in battle and his commanding presence among the people appeared to check all the right boxes. Even Samuel, though still unsure, dared to hope Saul might make something of himself—that is, until he defied a clear instruction from Samuel, who was continuing in his role of being the moral, religious conscience of the nation. The infraction Saul committed, although seemingly minor and perhaps even justifiable under the circumstances, was still indicative of a heart that was prone not to follow. By 1 Samuel 15, when the Bible captures another of Saul's lapses in character, Samuel knew exactly who he was dealing with, and it wasn't good. Maybe God was right after all. (Now *that's* a wacky idea!)

Samuel wouldn't be alive by the time Saul's reign came to an end, but he probably could have guessed it wasn't going to be awesome.

I will say, whenever Saul was confronted with his sin, his initial responses could sure sound like genuine repentance. "I have sinned," he said. "I have transgressed the commandment of the LORD" (1 Sam. 15:24). But those are empty words if you're just saying them and not following through. The bottom line is that Saul would never love God the way he should, and what God wanted was someone who would. In fact, God said he was going to choose "a man after his own heart" (1 Sam. 13:14). As Samuel said in disgust to Saul, "The LORD has torn the kingdom of Israel from you this day and has given it to a neighbor of yours, who is better than you" (1 Sam. 15:28).

The beginning of the end was clear, almost from the very beginning.

Therefore, Samuel sought another. Not a *perfect* man, but one whose heart was truly, purely, completely invested in everything he said and did.

Come to find out, though, this "man after God's own heart" wasn't even a man yet.

THE SHEPHERD BOY

King Saul, the big and tall, remains a vivid example of a timeless truth: "The LORD sees not as man sees: man looks on the outward appearance, but the LORD looks on the heart" (1 Sam. 16:7). Surprisingly though, even Samuel was susceptible to forgetting this spiritual reality. When the Lord led him to the home of a man named Jesse in Bethlehem, to seek God's replacement for the failed Saul experiment, he took one look at Jesse's oldest son and thought, *Here is king material if I ever saw it.* But the Lord said no to all seven of the strapping young sons that Jesse paraded past him.

This next part makes me laugh.

"Are all your sons here?" (v. 11). I imagine Jesse flustered and fidgeting, saying, "Yeah, I mean . . . no, I mean . . . yeah, there's *one* more, but . . ."

The other one—the last one—was the youngest one. And the reason Jesse hadn't thought to bring him in at first was because he was out in the fields tending to the livestock. But as soon as his dad sent for him and had him stand up to be examined, the Lord said to Samuel, "Arise, anoint him, for this is he" (v. 12).

Plot twist.

It's so like God to choose the unexpected.

Basically, God was anointing a kid to be king, but the kid wouldn't actually become a king until he was a grown man. Translation: "Hey, big boys. Remember how you mocked me, your kid brother, for skipping out on your gym trips and refusing to share your hair gel? Cool. I'm going to be your king one day."

Saul kept reigning with no knowledge of the fact that his successor had already been chosen. He did, however, realize his kingdom was being stripped away from him, and it was driving him crazy. Like, actually crazy. He became a madman, raging around and refusing to be comforted. So his servants suggested that he bring in a skilled musician to serenade him whenever he pointed to the really angry face on that chart they'd made for him. Turns out, one of the people on staff knew of a young man who was talented on the harp, and so Saul called in a favor.

Heyyyyyyy, Jesse? King of Israel here. Listen, I've kind of, uh . . . well, I've lost my mind, is what's happened, and I'm in need of some music therapy. I hear you've got a guy . . .

You'll never guess who was practicing his harp while his brothers were at the twenty-four-hour gym.

Seriously. SAUL WAS BEING CALMED DOWN BY THE GUY WHO WOULD TAKE HIS THRONE.

Ah, the irony.

And because it wasn't enough for David to have to drag his harp to the palace at Saul's whim, he also wrangled himself into some crazy situations along the way.

THE GIANT KILLER

David must have been on call one day, but instead of shoveling sheep dung in the fields, his dad sent him to the battlefront with a care package for three of David's big brothers who were soldiers in Saul's army. The battle they were currently fighting was against Israel's longtime rivals, the Philistines. And to make matters even worse (because we always love for that to happen), the Philistines had a guy who made an impression when he showed up. Like, all ten feet of him.

You may have heard of Goliath. Well these are his fifteen minutes of Bible fame, and it didn't go the way he was hoping it would.

Of course, no one was exactly offering to fight him (you know, because they were just SOLDIERS WHOSE JOB WAS TO FIGHT THE ENEMY), so David picked up a couple of rocks, whirled one around from his slingshot directly into Goliath's forehead, and watched the giant's body fall to the ground with a thud. I'm sure it made for all-cap headlines in the morning paper: "SHEPHERD-HARPIST KILLS GIANT; GAINS LOVE OF THE PEOPLE."

Remember, of course, that Saul was a bit . . . what's the word . . . unstable. And he was definitely not expecting his personal musician to start impressing the people that he ruled over. The whole situation was made more complex by the fact that Saul's son Jonathan and David had become besties. And Jonathan had some advice for David: RUN.

My dad's going to kill you. I'm assuming that means we're postponing racquetball practice.

After this, we see a series of events that follow the same pattern: Saul chases David. Saul tries to kill David (several times). Saul is unsuccessful. Every time. David has many chances to kill Saul, but doesn't take them.

But here's something interesting. During the time that David was trying to escape from Saul, he decided to put his thoughts into writing and composed a good bit of the book of Psalms. There are other authors, but David is pretty much the star. Take Psalm 59, for example. Listen to what he said, and see if it doesn't sound like a man on the run from his archenemy:

> Deliver me from those who work evil, and save me from bloodthirsty men. For behold, they lie in wait for my life; fierce men stir up strife against me. . . . Each evening they come back, howling like dogs and prowling about the city. There they are, bellowing with their mouths, with swords in their lips—for "Who," they think, "will hear us?" But you, O LORD, laugh at them . . . for you, O God, are my fortress. My God in his stead-fast love will meet me; God will let me look in triumph on my enemies. (vv. 2–3, 6–10)

He is feeling his feelings, isn't he?

Altogether, eight of the psalms reflect on David's experiences in running from Saul. And the rest, well, they give us an everyday selection of starters for our prayers and our praises.

Finally, David's old nemesis bit the bullet. More accurately, during another battle with the Philistines—as Saul sensed the tide turning against him, as he could feel the enemy closing in—the old coward deliberately fell on his own sword rather than be captured, taunted, and tortured.

And yet David, respectful of God's plans and purposes to the end, sang a hymn in tribute, not in triumph, over this first king to rule on the throne of Israel:

> "You daughters of Israel, weep over Saul, who clothed you luxuriously in scarlet, who put ornaments of gold on your apparel. How the mighty have fallen in the midst of the battle! . . . How the mighty have fallen, and the weapons of war perished!" (2 Sam. 1:24–25, 27)

KING DAVID

Customarily, of course, upon the death of a king—if they've not been overthrown by coup or conquered by invaders—the throne passes down from father to child. But three of Saul's sons, including brave and fearless Jonathan, were killed in the same battle that claimed their father's life. One son, however—with the rocking name Ish-bosheth— did survive, and a faction of loyalists attempted to establish him as Saul's rightful successor.

For seven and a half years, amid this vacuum of ambition and infighting, the reach of David's kingdom was confined to the southern tribes only, where he set up operations among his home base in territory assigned to the tribe of Judah. But when Ish-bosheth (THAT IS A LOT TO MONOGRAM) was murdered by zealous assassins, the northern tribes fell into disarray. Seeking stability, they appealed to David to fill their leadership void as well.

And that's how *all* the tribes came together into one big, happy (though, as always, rather contentious) family, known to biblical history as the United Kingdom. Not the

"Duchess Kate" United Kingdom. It's simply a name that signifies the opposite of what the nation had been and of what they would later become again: the Divided Kingdom.

In quick succession, David captured the city of Jerusalem and made it his capital. He subdued all the enemies around them. Then with great pageantry he brought the ark of the covenant out of its temporary home in the tabernacle, desiring to build a glorious, permanent place for it and for the worship of God. In a temple. In Jerusalem.

That's how "a man after [God's] own heart" would think, don't you agree? As he said to the prophet Nathan, "I dwell in a house of cedar, but the ark of God dwells in a tent" (2 Sam. 7:2). Didn't sound right to him. Gotta love that kind of humble, worshipful spirit, wanting to build a lasting place where God could abide with his people forever and receive their obedient, grateful praise.

But Nathan, after stepping away from that conversation—which in the moment, of course, had seemed to be a tremendous idea on David's part—found in the overnight hours that he was hearing from God a different word. God's plan for David, like God's plan for Moses, did not involve the leader of Israel seeing with his own eyes the culmination of what the Lord had begun under his leadership. But just as God possessed something even better in mind for Moses (a one-way ticket to the ultimate Promised Land), he also had something better in mind for David. His son Solomon would build the temple based on what David had begun to prepare.

And best of all, David's kingdom would last forever.

Yes, you are tying it together now. The *coming deliverer* of Genesis 3 who would crush the head of the serpent is the same *coming descendant* in Genesis 12 who would bless the world through Abraham's family line, which we now see is the *coming son* who will reign on David's throne forever and ever and ever.

Another *covenant* promise from God.

And though David was understandably disappointed at hearing from Nathan that the temple would not be his own personal legacy project to undertake, he was reverent about it. He deferred to God's decisions without arguing or complaining. He cried out, praising the Lord:

> "What more can David say to you? For you know your servant, O Lord God! Because of your promise, and according to your own heart, you have brought about all this greatness, to make your servant know it. Therefore you are great, O Lord God. For there is none like you, and there is no God besides you." (2 Sam. 7:20–22)

I just love David and his heart so much. Don't you?

Take, for example, the incident with Bathsheba (the woman taking a bath, which makes her name easier to remember). To say the least, David made a questionable decision there. And by "questionable," I mean, he saw a naked woman bathing on her roof, slept with her, and then had her husband put on the front lines of the battle to kill him. But as bad as it was—and it was both genuinely hedonistic and genuinely heinous—he genuinely grieved his sin and repented in a genuine, humble way.

David fell because any of us can fall. The reason he could be called a man after God's own heart was not because he never dreamed of sinning; he was a man after God's own heart because he kept coming back to him.

Words alone, as we witnessed with Saul, can never provide enough smoke screen for a heart that's still rebellious on the underside. But David's words, though similar in nature to Saul's, tell us something to indicate that David's sorrow, by notable contrast, was more than skin-deep. He knew what he'd done and knew it was wrong. "My sin is ever before me," he said (Ps. 51:3)—sin that he'd committed directly in God's face. No selfish excuses. No elaborate passing of blame. *I have sinned against a holy God, and my spirit is grieved because of it.*

This next part hits a little close to home for me, so I want to take a second to talk about it. Because of David's sin, God allowed his firstborn child with Bathsheba to die. There's no confusion; this is a causation incident. That's true for David's situation. But for us, we must remember we are on the other side of the cross now—where our sins are paid for by Christ, not ourselves. In the gospel, the primary person dealing with the loss of a son (temporarily) is God himself, when his Son took on the sin of the world and paid for it on the cross of Calvary. So when it comes to our own losses in life, yes, they are sometimes self-inflicted, natural consequences of our sin. (For example, if we continue to hurt a friend, they will probably cut ties with us. That's not God's punishment; that's a natural consequence. We caused it, and the consequence followed.) However, other times, our losses are not self-inflicted by our sin, and we didn't cause them. One of the most dangerous things we can do is assume causation when there is absolutely no reason to believe it's the case. The thing is, we're human, and the first place we often go is, "What did I do to cause this? God is punishing me because I did *x, y, z* . . ."

Hear the word of the Lord: "He has not dealt with us as our sins deserve or repaid us according to our iniquities" (Ps. 103:10 csb). Limiting God to rigid acts of retaliation is a misread of Scripture and, more important, a poor understanding of his fatherly heart.

I speak boldly here because, as someone who has lost a child to death, I've been the victim of this kind of thinking. I've felt its wounding words, its condemning tones, coming at me at all hours. I would lie awake at night after we found out our daughter Audrey wasn't going to survive, recounting mistakes I had made, camping out on the notion that I was being punished for my sins.

If you've struggled with this kind of cause-and-effect assumption, I can talk with you as someone who's been there, and someone who could easily go there again in my darker moments. But I've learned from his Word and from my experience with him that our God is good. He is not out to destroy his children. He deals with us personally, not prescriptively, because he knows us better than anyone else—knows exactly what we need. And, ultimately, he deals with us in Christ. Like any good father, he is a lot more interested in seeing us healed and restored than buried under the weight of our sins. That's why he sent his Son in the first place.

That's why I'm not surprised to see, after the heartbreak of this season in David's life, the Lord met his painful gaze with a dose of fresh blessing.

Though one child could never replace another, God did bring joy back into David's household.

Another son.

SOLOMON

David's relationship with God had been restored, but it didn't turn the United Kingdom into the Magic Kingdom. Another of David's sons, Absalom, seething with resentment toward his father, came dangerously close to stealing the throne for himself. The king was forced to flee the city to escape the clutches of his kid's conspiracy. But Absalom ended up being killed instead, when his long, flowing hair *(Hey, Fabio!)* became entangled in a low-hanging tree branch as his horse sprinted out from under him. David wanted Absalom spared, but his men—going against orders—cut him down with three javelins to the heart. David regained the throne, but with a heavy, fatherly loss.

The time ultimately came, though, for David to implement his own succession plan. And although another son, Adonijah, sought to set himself up as king (these people will turn on their own father at the drop of a dime), David's friend Nathan intervened along with Bathsheba to secure David's choice of Solomon as royal heir.

With his dying words, David charged Solomon to be strong, to be a man—to always remain a man of God—"walking in his ways and keeping his statutes, his commandments, his rules, and his testimonies, as it is written in the Law of Moses, that you may prosper in all that you do and wherever you turn" (1 Kings 2:3). And Solomon, on many occasions, showed the seriousness with which he received his father's counsel. When God came to him in the first days of his reign, offering to give him whatever his heart most desired, Solomon famously asked for *wisdom,* more than long life or wealth or domination over his enemies. Could maybe call him a kiss-up. But pleased with Solomon's response, the Lord promised him all those other things as well.

In many ways his reign could be considered Israel's golden age, a forty-year era of peace and prosperity. The depth of his insights caused his reputation to spread far and wide, so that people traveled hundreds of miles to come ask him questions about the meaning of life. He compiled the wise teachings of the *Proverbs* as well as the *Song of Solomon*, a love poem that celebrates the joy and commitment of wedded love (there are no chapters about naked women on rooftops), while illustrating the passionate loyalty of God's love for his people. He may even have been the author of the biblical book of *Ecclesiastes*. Although if so, he was certainly an old, less hopeful man by the time he wrote it. Ecclesiastes is a bit surprising among biblical literature because of its somewhat cynical view on life's purpose and human endeavors, but one thing is for sure. It puts us in our place when it comes to the futility of striving after things that just aren't going to last forever.

In addition, Solomon completed construction on the magnificent temple. And the prayerful, worshipful extravagance of its dedication ceremony was surpassed only by the breathtaking experience of God's presence among them.

> As soon as Solomon finished his prayer, fire came down from heaven and consumed the burnt offering and the sacrifices, and the glory of the LORD filled the temple. And the priests could not enter the house of the LORD, because the glory of the LORD filled the LORD's house. (2 Chron. 7:1–2)

While Solomon gave clear evidence at times that he "loved the LORD, walking in the statutes of David his father," he also "sacrificed and made offerings at the high places" (1 Kings 3:3). Like his father, he had a love for the ladies, and he took many, *many* wives for himself, a large number of whom came from pagan cultures and who seduced his heart away from the one true God (apple, meet tree).

So just as the eleventh chapter of 2 Samuel represents a downward pivot in the life of King David, the eleventh chapter of 1 Kings delineates a similar point of descent in the life of his son. "Solomon loved many foreign women, along with the daughter of Pharaoh" (1 Kings 11:1). And needless to say, this didn't go over too well with God.

Of course, he would not abandon his covenant, the establishment of David's royal line as an everlasting kingdom. We're soon to see King Jesus step into that place of highest honor. But this kingdom that had become united under the reigns of the first three kings would splinter in half—into a Divided Kingdom—upon the death of Solomon.

- The Northern Kingdom, consisting of ten tribes, would be known as *Israel*.
- The Southern Kingdom, consisting of Judah and Benjamin, was called *Judah*.

And if you're curious about where all of this happens in the Bible, you're going to need to stay tuned. For now, I just want you to know the story, and then we'll get into all that later. Do you feel like you've got somewhat of a handle on what's happened so far? If not, just know that we're going to do another recap as soon as the next chapter starts, and you're going to be in a prime position to meet the fine folks we call prophets. Like the judges and kings, their job was to warn the Israelites to shape up. How do you think that will turn out? Well, let's see.

MEDITERRANEAN SEA

SEA OF GALILEE

Samaria   **ISRAEL**

Jerusalem·
Bethlehem

DEAD SEA

JUDAH

Eastern
Desert

THE DIVIDED KINGDOM

Chapter 10

YOU MIGHT WANT TO LISTEN TO THIS
The Prophets and the Exile

 For our purposes here, I'm not reaching as far back as Abraham or even Moses. We've spent a lot of time on their stories already. Instead, I'm restarting things around the time of Samuel. Do you remember him? Good. Some of it will be review, which will make you feel smart. And I'm glad you feel that way because now you're going to use that confidence to learn some new stuff. And if any of it looks confusing, I promise you'll get the hang of it as we go.

1. The time of the judges ended, and the people wanted a king.
2. At that time, the twelve tribes were kind of doing their own thing and weren't a nation.
3. Saul was anointed as the first king. It didn't go well. He needed a therapist.
4. David was chosen as the next king.
5. David was credited with uniting the tribes into a single nation (the United Kingdom).
6. David captured Jerusalem, made it the capital, and began to plan a majestic temple for the worship of God. It would

give the ark of the covenant a permanent home instead of being in a traveling tent.

7. God told David he hadn't called him
to build the temple, that he'd assigned
the job instead to his son Solomon, who
would eventually take David's place as
king.

8. Solomon built a spectacular temple.

9. Solomon, through lavish living and
his many, many, MANY foreign wives,
compromised his heart and accom-
modated their worship of idols. This
resulted in the United Kingdom being
split into two separate kingdoms: the
Northern Kingdom (Israel) and the
Southern Kingdom (Judah).

*Excuse me for stepping in here for a sec. This is sort of
where we left off at the end of the last chapter. So now, here
we go—all new territory in through here. Ready? Of course
you are.*

10. Both nations had a bunch of terrible
kings for hundreds of years. It wasn't
awesome. God raised up prophets—first
to warn the northern part, then to warn
the southern part—eventually warning *all* the parts of impending defeat if
they didn't shape up. But they weren't
the kind of kids who stay on their mats
during circle time.

11. Israel was ultimately conquered by
Assyria (the bad boys of the eighth
century BC), and Judah was defeated
by Babylon (the bad boys of the sixth

century BC). The Babylonians destroyed Solomon's amazing temple in the process.

12. Both of these invaders decided to haul off a bunch of the defeated people as slaves, which left a lot of folks displaced from the Promised Land. This is called the "Exile" because, you know, it was an exile.

13. The Northern Kingdom never reorganized, but God brought the people of Judah back home after seventy years so they could reestablish the nation.

14. The first captives who were released began to build a new temple in Jerusalem, and they were all sad because it was nowhere near as grand as the first.

15. Then guess what: *more* prophets! They said it wouldn't be like this forever (this sad, incomplete feeling) because—good news!—a Redeemer was on the way.

16. I don't exactly have a 16, but congratulations for paying attention.

I can think of at least two common threads that run through this portion of the Bible story, same as they ran through all the parts of the story we talked about before. The first is that sin and rebellion inevitably result in painful consequences. The people's refusal to stay united in their devotion to God not only split their own nation in two, but eventually scattered them to the four winds. They became slaves to their enemies rather than living in peace, living in victory.

But then there's another thread: *God responds*. We've seen this one all along as well. God comes looking. God comes saving. God comes trying to talk some sense into us. So he raised up people from all different backgrounds and called them to preach to the people and warn them about the consequences that would come if they continued to sin and rebel against God. We're going to see them all over the place at different points in time, but just so you know, there were two kinds of prophets: major prophets and minor prophets. This doesn't have anything to do with their importance; it's just a reference to the length of their books.

The prophet's job was simply to bring the message of God to the people, and this was a new way of communicating because up until now, God had spoken to individuals through burning bushes, etc. But this was for all of the people. The prophets were simply the mouthpiece for God, and as you can imagine, they were not everybody's vote for prom king.

The point is that even though a lot of what they say sounds like gloom and doom, the heart of what God was doing was actually beautiful: he didn't want to cut off communication with them even when they were running from him.

Another big thing we learn from the prophets is that God really cares about the marginalized, vulnerable, and oppressed. If you've ever struggled to believe God really cares about the evil in the world, the prophets show you he does. He has some hard words in there for those who are pompous in their wrongdoing, those who act like they're in the right while they're harming people everywhere they go. He doesn't overlook this stuff, he doesn't find it funny, and—what's more—he starts with his own people when it comes to dishing out judgment.

He doesn't show partiality the way humans do. In our world, people are quick to point out the sins of others, demanding justice, all the while covering up the sins in their own camp. But through the prophets, we see that God goes the opposite route. He starts with his own people. In this way, although the prophets can be intense to read, take care to remember that this is the Bible's way of showing us that God really, really, really does care about wrongdoing, injustice, and hypocrisy—outside of his own people, yes, but also and especially *within* them.

The prophets spoke both about things that were happening in real time as well as things that would happen in the future. Those events, along with the prophets' ministries, sort of play out across the Bible in three or four waves. We're going to pick up where we left off with Solomon, just after the United Kingdom fell apart.

WAVE ONE: BEFORE THE FIRST INVASION

So we've got two kingdoms now: the North and the South, right? Feel free to look back if you can't quite remember what they were called. Let's start by talking about the Northern Kingdom's adventures, shall we? There were three prophets who ministered there before the Assyrians conquered them. First up? Jonah.

JONAH

Okay, so when my oldest two girls (identical twins) were around three, I decided to recreate the story of Jonah because I am the kind of mom who likes to make sure I have a tangible example of stories in Scripture every single day. I never miss one ever. And also, my kids had memorized the Bible, so there's that.

Joking.

In reality, there was only this *one occasion* where I put blue dye in their bathwater, told them the whole story (complete with candles that I blew out once Jonah ended up in the fish), and then gave them a solid sermon on the moral lesson behind the story and how we can apply it to our lives. Why do I mention it? Because I did it that once. *Once.* But if I write it here, you'll imagine I'm the kind of mother I would like to imagine I am.

I did not, however, include the background of the story of Jonah, which was mostly related to the fact that I didn't know it. But now I do, and I would love to share it with you.

Here's the thing. We always picture Jonah disobeying and getting swallowed by a whale (or at least by a "great fish," it says—remember I talked to you about that?) and then spit out because of God's grace. That's not inaccurate, but the rest of the story makes it more interesting. Jonah's assignment from God was to travel to a city called Nineveh, which was in Assyria. Remember now, these were his enemies and also the folks that would eventually conquer Israel. They were not nice people. So instead of going where God told him to go, he went the opposite direction. He didn't want God to give them grace; he wanted them to suffer.

Alas, God convicted him to go back, which Jonah did. And with just a few words from Jonah's mouth, the whole city of Nineveh repented.

But Jonah was a stubborn fella, and he decided that God's plan was still frustrating, so he sat on the edge of town under a tree, sulking while telling God he shouldn't have rescued them. "Hey, God, thanks for the whole vomiting-me-out-of-the-fish thing, but I'm going to need to sit over here and pray they all change their minds and ignore you. Good talk."

And now we're going to meet Mr. Amos. He's kind of a fruit guy.

AMOS

Amos was what you might call a lay preacher, not a professional. He referred to himself instead as "a herdsman and a dresser of sycamore figs. But the LORD took me from following the flock," he said, "and the LORD said to me, 'Go, prophesy to my people Israel'" (Amos 7:14–15). I don't know if you've ever read any of the Amelia Bedelia books, but I'm just saying she would have had a field day with the whole "dressing figs" thing.

Amos spoke in tough, honest terms. And who was he talking to? Right, the Northern Kingdom. And when was this happening? You got it, friend—ahead of the Assyrian invasion. He told them if they refused to hear the truth about their revolting behavior and heed God's warnings of impending judgment, their kids would die, their land would be divided up, their wireless signal would be hopelessly unreliable, "and Israel shall surely go into exile" (Amos 7:17). Well, that's encouraging.

But they had a choice; they always had a choice. They just didn't pick the right one.

HOSEA

Hosea, it might be said, presented an even more compelling case for change. He made his own life a visible symbol of what God desired to do for his people. At the Lord's direction, he married a known prostitute who, unsurprisingly, continued to prove unfaithful to him after their marriage, running after other men, eventually becoming their slave. And yet Hosea, in a stunning example of love and grace, obeyed God's command to "go again, love a woman who is loved by another man and is an adulteress, even as the LORD loves the children of Israel, though they turn to other gods" (Hosea 3:1). He approached the men who were

165

selling his wife on the slave block and paid the price to redeem her from a lifetime of hopeless bondage.

It's one of the most endearing pictures in all the Bible. Hosea's book is like a sermon where his own pursuit of his cheating wife is the sermon illustration. And in hearing it, in seeing it, the people had no doubt who each role in the story represented. The prostitute was playing the part of Israel, and Hosea was in the role of God, loving them in spite of their mistakes and sin. But despite God's depth of devotion to unfaithful Israel, they would not accept life on his terms.

ISAIAH

Isaiah's book is the longest, and we're going to be referring to it often when we move into the days of Christ. The reason for that is because while he was speaking to the people in Judah hundreds of years before Jesus was born, he was already speaking of the coming Savior. He was also warning them about the danger the Assyrians and Babylonians posed, but as usual, his audience wasn't all that moved by his suggestions.

MICAH

Micah, too, prophesied to the Southern Kingdom (Judah), which was a nation that considered itself immune to God's judgment. They felt as though their wicked practices could never really be bad enough that God would call them to account for it. Micah was pretty specific with them, reciting the words that God had given him: "Zion shall be plowed as a field; Jerusalem shall become a heap of ruins" (Micah 3:12). He told them the mountain where the temple now stood would one day be just a hillside with some scrubby trees and too-tall grass. That's not really a subtle warning. These people were well aware of the fact that they were sinning. They just didn't care.

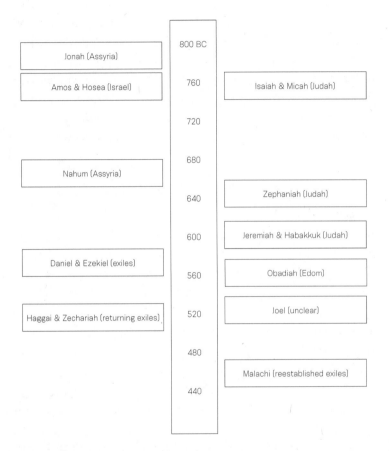

OLD TESTAMENT PROPHETS: LIFETIMES AND AUDIENCES

But both Micah and Isaiah point to a day when things will be set right. They tell of the way God will "cast all our sins into the depths of the sea. You will show faithfulness to Jacob and steadfast love to Abraham, as you have sworn to our fathers from the days of old" (Micah 7:19–20).

And may I just say, I love seeing our old friends Abraham and Jacob reappearing way out here in the latter pages of the Old Testament. God's long-ago covenant was still resonating and in force just as powerfully as when he first presented it to them years ago under a star-specked sky.

Now that the Northern tribes had been defeated, we're going to see if the prophecies made to the South would be taken any more seriously. I mean, they watched prophecy come true to the North, so I'm sure they'll whip into shape.

WAVE TWO: BEFORE THE SECOND INVASION

There were five prophets trying to convince Judah to get it together before they were also defeated, and they were the life of the party.

NAHUM

Remember the story of Jonah and the way he tried to avoid preaching to the Assyrians? Well, Nahum is kind of a sequel to the prophecy of Jonah. He was prophesying against Nineveh as well, but he wasn't trying to bring them back to God. He was telling them that what goes around comes around.

HABAKKUK

Now we have to imagine that somewhere along here, there would be someone wondering if God was really for His people. And Habakkuk is the guy. He asked God the kind of imponderable questions a person of faith still asks when faced with the decay of their nation around them. *Why aren't you hearing our prayers, God? Why aren't you doing something to stop this, God? How much longer can we hold out, God, if you don't come down here and help us?*

But in the end, he knew that even if the worst of all scenarios came about, even if the Babylonians really did come along and crush them, "yet I will rejoice in the LORD; I will take joy in the God of my salvation" (Hab. 3:18). Good for you, Habakkuk.

ZEPHANIAH

Zephaniah is a hoot. He loved talking about a quickly approaching event: "a day of distress and anguish, a day of ruin and devastation, a day of darkness and gloom, a day of clouds and thick darkness, a day of trumpet blast and battle cry" (Zeph. 1:15–16). So, basically, it's like a vacation.

Yet as with all the other prophets of this period, God punctuated his words of doom with promises of hope. His purpose behind these hard days was not to punish his people but to purify them, to make them shine as an example of how deeply God's grace can reach. In time he would prove to them, even in their most difficult moments, even when they'd find it hardest to believe, the beautiful words Zephaniah gave us: "The LORD your God is in your midst, a mighty one who will save; he will rejoice over you with gladness; he will quiet you by his love; he will exult over you with loud singing" (v. 17).

OBADIAH

Obadiah's book is the shortest of all—just *one chapter*—so I'll keep his summary quick as well. He probably did his prophesying right as the Babylonians were overrunning Jerusalem, preaching not to the Jews but to the nearby people of Edom, who were all sitting around celebrating the downfall of Jerusalem. Obadiah told them that they would be punished for it. He also told them that the people of Israel would be back there one day, so they might want to cancel the after-party.

JEREMIAH

Jeremiah was a crier. Which is probably why he's often referred to as "the weeping prophet." He mourned the downfall of Jerusalem and the destruction of the temple. And with the Babylonian attack clearly imminent, he also mourned that so many of his countrymen were being led astray by *false* prophets, who were going around telling everybody, "'Peace, peace,' when there is no peace" (Jer. 8:11). Because here's just the truth of it. Remember back in Deuteronomy, when Moses declared God's instructions to the people, giving them the choice between life and death?—life if they obeyed? death if they rebelled? No matter what their religious leaders were telling them today, Jeremiah said, this is what God had been saying all along:

> "I solemnly warned your fathers when I
> brought them up out of the land of Egypt,
> warning them persistently, even to this day,
> saying, Obey my voice. Yet they did not obey
> or incline their ear, but everyone walked in
> the stubbornness of his evil heart. Therefore
> I brought upon them all the words of this
> covenant, which I commanded them to do,
> but they did not." (Jer. 11:7–8)

It's not a hundred percent certain, but many people think Jeremiah also wrote another book—*Lamentations*—after the destruction of Jerusalem actually happened. It all just seemed so final, their sins so unforgivable: "How lonely sits the city that was full of people! How like a widow has she become, she who was great among the nations! She who was a princess among the provinces has become a slave" (Lam. 1:1).

After that he ordered takeout and watched Hallmark movies.

But have no fear. One day he will be credited with one of the most well-known verses in Scripture. You know he cried from heaven when he found that out.

WAVE THREE: DURING THE EXILE

In Jeremiah 25, God said after seventy years he was going to punish the king of Babylon and bring his people home. Have you ever heard this verse before?—"I know the plans I have for you, declares the LORD, plans for welfare and not for evil, to give you a future and a hope" (Jer. 29:11). We rightly apply these same words to ourselves and our own lives today, but their original intent was to encourage the Jews who'd been taken far away from home, telling them that Babylon was not going to be the end for them. Now when you see it embroidered on baby wall art, you'll think . . . *Yessss!* . . . *That's what he said to the Jews who would return to Jerusalem after being captured by Babylon!*

Judah's captivity—their *exile*—would last seventy years, just as God had said. But it wouldn't last forever. They *did* have a hope and a future. In the meantime, they were supposed to set up shop in Babylon for a while. And yet even during this time, as they remained temporarily uprooted in Babylon, God continued to raise up other prophets to speak his word to them.

EZEKIEL

Ezekiel seems the most eccentric of the prophets because instead of just speaking his messages in words, he often acted them out, literally staged what he was trying to say. He is sometimes referred to as "the charades prophet." No, that's a lie, but I totally would've chosen him for my team. He did things, like, scratch the outline of Jerusalem on an adobe brick and then play army against it, or dig underneath a wall in his house to show how the people had tried escaping the city before it fell. That's actually not a joke. These were real pastimes of his, according to the Bible.

Ezekiel can be a tricky book to follow and definitely has a hard edge and tone to it. He didn't really leave anyone just hanging out and laughing over dinner. It was all so depressing. Still, he's probably best known for his vision of a valley of dry, dead bones that suddenly rattled back to life when God breathed his Spirit into them. For even though the exile had been a death blow, "I will open your graves and raise you from your graves, O my people" (Ezek. 37:12).

So let's pull the lens back for a quick second. When you read that verse, do you know who God is referring to as a valley of dead bones that will come back to life? I wonder if you ever knew that all the rattling was the sound of Israel beginning to breathe again. But not yet. We've still got to get through this whole Babylonian captivity thing.

DANIEL

Daniel, of course, is probably better known than all the other prophets, primarily because of the fascinating stories his book contains, like the three men who survived a fiery furnace and, who can forget, Daniel and the lions' den. I want to take this opportunity to confess that I've dealt with flannel board envy throughout my adult life. I didn't grow up in the church, and I GUARANTEE other kids got to see these stories smacked on there. Probably had a fun activity and worksheet to go along with it. It's fine. I'm over it. Can't you tell?

But don't miss the basics of what was happening. These aren't just flannel board stories that float around in space. They're real events backed up by real history and real documents. Daniel and these other three Jewish guys had been taken captive by the Babylonians, where King Nebuchadnezzar was in charge. You have some context now, right? They refused to bow down to their captors' gods, which ended up getting them in various versions of hot water.

Then while Daniel was still in captivity, Babylon fell and the Persians took over. (Persia was the original name of the country we now know as Iran.) That's how the Babylonian Empire got swallowed up into—*tada!*— the Persian Empire. Anyway, that's why the king in the "Daniel and the Lions' Den" story is the king of Persia, King Darius, and no longer our old King Nezzie of Babylon. That's a lot, I know. Stick with me, though, because this next part is so cool.

When the Persians took over Babylon, the victorious king was a man known as Cyrus II or Cyrus the Great. Well, listen to what the prophet Isaiah said (remember Isaiah?), like, two or three hundred years before:

> Thus says the LORD, your Redeemer, who formed you from the womb: "I am the LORD, who made all things, who alone stretched out the heavens, who spread out the earth by myself . . . who says of Jerusalem, 'She shall be inhabited,' and of the cities of Judah, 'They shall be built, and I will raise up their ruins' . . . who says of Cyrus, 'He is my shepherd, and he shall fulfill all my purpose'; saying of Jerusalem, 'She shall be built,' and of the temple, 'Your foundation shall be laid.'" (Isa. 44:24, 26b, 28)

Okay, whoa whoa whoa whoa whoa. Isaiah, centuries before, when Jerusalem was already built and fully populated, spoke of a time when Jerusalem would be *rebuilt* and *repopulated*. "What is he even talking about?" the people of his day must have wondered. But did you catch the name of the guy—again, written hundreds of years prior—who God said would give the order for Jerusalem to be put back on its foundations?

See? The joy of prophecy. This was hundreds of years before Jerusalem would be ruined, before the Jews would be snatched away, and Isaiah was already telling us the NAME of the person who would send them home.

So as it turns out, a king finally released the Jews, allowing them to return to their homeland, rebuild their lives, and live freely again—which would be the end of the Exile. Praise be. And now, onto the time period after the Israelites returned to their land.

WAVE FOUR: AFTER THE EXILE

We've got three or four more prophets coming up, but before we get to them, I'm going to slide in a couple of other books that fall within this time period. We mentioned that the Jews were beginning to head back to Jerusalem, and that's what these next books are going to zoom in on.

EZRA AND NEHEMIAH

The books of Ezra and Nehemiah both talk about the same time period when the Jews were allowed to start traveling home. But things in Judah weren't exactly how they were when they left. Let's move on to the next wave of folks who returned, and then we'll be in prime position to head back to our last few prophets.

HAGGAI AND ZECHARIAH

The first bunch came home with permission from Cyrus to get to work reconstructing the temple. But while they were wildly enthusiastic to get started, they quickly grew discouraged by their slow progress.

Thankfully, Haggai and Zechariah were on the ground with these guys, urging their fellow citizens to show some spunk here. God reminded them through Haggai not to think that the reason they'd been able to come back to Jerusalem was simply because of the gracious generosity of Cyrus the king. I mean, it was lovely of him to send them back, but this was all part of the covenant that God had made with their forefathers "when you came out of Egypt" (Hag. 2:5). This was big. Too big to be sitting around feeling sorry for themselves when they ought to be hauling and building stuff.

Or as Zechariah put it, "Do not be like your fathers," who heard the earlier prophets urging them to live up to their heritage but who "did not hear or pay attention" (Zech. 1:4). God had given this new generation the chance to put their trust and faith in the Lord, the way their fathers had failed to do, and to honor him with their courageous obedience.

So, this first group of Israelites finally got the temple built, but it was nowhere near as beautiful as Solomon's. They called it Zerubbabel's Temple because it was such a catchy name. Actually, he was just the leader of this pack that had come home from Babylon to Jerusalem so he called dibs.

News of the temple's completion ignited the *second* wave of exiles. Ezra himself led this group, which resulted in restoring worship practices at the temple, the way they hadn't been done in years. A *third* party of travelers arrived later with Nehemiah, with whom they famously rebuilt the broken-down walls around the city. Nehemiah faithfully, courageously stood down the opposition from the local sheriff and his deputies, rallied his men, and got 'er done.

We're getting close now. Just a couple more prophets, and then we will move along to "post-exile fashion trends."

JOEL

The prophet Joel didn't leave any clues behind to help us decode the time zone in which he lived and worked. All we know is that he reported on a withering plague of locusts which he attributed to the judgment of God. And he left us with a beautifully worded promise from the Lord that says, to those of us who've sometimes felt our own lives reduced to stubs and twigs, "I will restore to you the years that the swarming locust has eaten" (Joel 2:25). I can't wait until we get into the New Testament because there's another guy who likes locusts, and he's delightful in spite of his odd keto diet.

ESTHER

Okay, Esther wasn't a prophet, *but I've got to get her in here someway.* She has the coolest story, and it falls right around here chronology-wise. It's a lush story of palace intrigue, petty grudges, and the unmistakable providence of God. The events that the book of Esther describes took place in Persia, after many of the Jews had returned to their homeland, and yet some of them had chosen to stay back and assimilate into Persian culture.

Esther was a young Jewish girl who, against all odds, was chosen as queen of the empire, and whose uncommon wisdom and bravery—traits she didn't even know she possessed—thwarted a pre-Nazi attempt at exterminating the entire Jewish race. Her cousin became aware of the plot, and at one point said to her, "Who knows whether you have not come to the kingdom for such a time as this?" (Esther 4:14), to use her influence as a way of perhaps stopping it.

I love it. It was risky to talk to her husband about it because she was not allowed to visit him unless she was summoned. Those were just the rules for approaching the king. He could kill her on the spot if she came without being requested.

Clearly, this was a man who liked to be in control and didn't like to be surprised. He'd already excommunicated his first wife for not coming when he *had* called her, sooooo . . . what would he do with Esther for approaching him at a moment when he *hadn't*? She was probably facing the same kind of realistic options. Either death or exile. Yet she went to the king in spite of her fear, and waited to see if he would hold out his scepter to indicate that she could approach him.

Last Father's Day, you couldn't even *find* a scepter. Sold out EVERYWHERE. That was a downer, because I had big plans for my husband, Todd, to be able to summon me at will. I've always said that the way to a man's heart is through a scepter.

Let's just say I wouldn't have made it to the honeymoon.

She was willing to die for her people, but the king held out his scepter and allowed her to speak. She told the king that someone on his staff was plotting to kill all of her people, so he intervened and let's just say things didn't turn out super well for the guy in charge of all the plotting. It didn't help that he was actually the king's head official. The extinction plan was thwarted because of Esther's courage, and to this day Jewish people celebrate this event in a festival known as Purim, where they read the entire book of Esther and insert different cheers and commentary throughout.

MALACHI

Before I tell you about Malachi (because he is so awesome that he deserves to close this chapter out), allow me an OCD moment, will you? Remember the list I made for you? The one we started the chapter with? I just want to be sure you know where all that history is told, which served as the backdrop for the prophets and their day jobs. I think I can do it with *one* more list, with one more walk through the history books of the Old Testament. It's getting real now. You're becoming an official Bible expert.

- 1 Samuel covers the birth of Samuel through the death of Saul
- 2 Samuel tells about the actions of David as king
- 1 Kings 1–11 is taken up with the reign of Solomon
- 1 Kings 12 marks the end of the unified kingdom
- From there to the end of 2 Kings is the story of the divided kingdom

So, what about Chronicles, Angie? Ah, you're in for a treat. The first and second books of Chronicles happen at the same time as *2 Samuel* and *1 and 2 Kings*. See? You already know it. The only difference is that the Chronicles focus more on the *religious* history wrapped up in these events, and the books of Samuel and Kings focus more on the *political* history.

All I'm saying is, if you were feeling even further behind by not knowing what happened in the books of 1 and 2 Chronicles—*don't*! They just give more detail on things you've gotten under your belt already. It's all good.

We can just sit here now and think about Malachi.

If I've said that once, I've said it a thousand times.

By the time of Malachi, the Jews had been back in their homeland for around a hundred years. They'd gone through a cycle of encouraging revival. Their temple was back on its foundation; many of the same fixtures and treasures that Nebuchadnezzar had stolen were now back where they belonged. A national life that their parents and grandparents had thought was gone forever had been restored to a state of normalcy—purer than it had actually been before.

But human nature, you know. What does it always do? Malachi came along at a time when the zeal for staying true to this God who'd brought them back from the dustbin of history had begun to ebb. They'd returned to their apathetic ways. As the Lord revealed earlier through Jeremiah: "The heart is deceitful above all things, and desperately sick; who can understand it?" (Jer. 17:9). IT'S JEREMIAH'S BIRTHDAY, GUYS! LET'S BUY HIM SOME MORE HANDKERCHIEFS.

Malachi, however, standing in the fading light of a culture slipping back into spiritual darkness, held his prophetic microphone to God's lips before everything went black. *Someone was coming,* the Lord said. Despite all their sin, all their disobedience, all their forgetfulness, and all their apathy, nothing could prevent God from continuing to seek his unfaithful bride. He keeps his word and loves his people with a ferocity that defies logic.

The biblical light was about to go dark for four hundred years, the blank space between what we call the Old and New Testaments. Yet from somewhere deep within that darkness, when all hope would seem lost again, God announced through his final prophet: "The sun of righteousness shall rise with healing in its wings" (Mal. 4:2).

This message, actually—despite all the other messages the prophets were called by God to communicate—is really what they were ultimately driving at. After all the chaos and cycles of sin and rejection, there would be a light. Life that had been so black and white would one day erupt in full color.

> "The Lord himself will give you a sign.
> Behold, the virgin shall conceive and bear
> a son, and shall call his name Immanuel."
> (Isa. 7:14)

A baby, born to a virgin, is coming?

> You, O Bethlehem Ephrathah, who are too
> little to be among the clans of Judah, from
> you shall come forth for me one who is to be
> ruler in Israel, whose coming forth is from
> old, from ancient days. (Mic. 5:2)

He will come from the tribe of Judah?

> Of the increase of his government and of
> peace there will be no end, on the throne of
> David and over his kingdom, to establish it
> and to uphold it with justice and with righ-
> teousness. (Isa. 9:7)

He will come from the line of David?
Oh, Israel, your King is coming for you.

He has never stopped loving you for one moment. And
when you meet this One that the world has been waiting
for, the mystery of his love will take on flesh and bear a
cross for his beloved.

> He was pierced for our transgressions; he
> was crushed for our iniquities; upon him
> was the chastisement that brought us peace,
> and with his wounds we are healed. (Isa.
> 53:5)

Long ago, the prophetic words of God's covenant
spilled into a starry night. And now, under the same cover
of night, the covenant would speak again.

This time, in the cry of a Baby.

Chapter 11

AND THE WEAVER
BECAME FLESH
Jesus

The Messiah King. The Suffering Servant. Our Redeemer.

Jesus, the Christ.

The entire Old Testament has been leading up to this moment, when the hero of the story—the weaver of the story—would come to us clothed in flesh and swaddled in blankets. Every encounter we've read, every person and problem we've met so far, has been like an arrow pointing us to Jesus.

Because whether any of those people from ancient generations knew it or not, he is what they'd been waiting their entire lives for . . . the entirety of all history for. Which makes me think it's a good time to flip back again to that spread containing all the main symbols of Bible history (page 14) and revisit the ones that most clearly reveal why Jesus, and only Jesus, could keep this *Woven* story from completely unraveling.

Take it all the way back to the beginning. The Fall, happening almost instantly after Creation, made the future already impossible. Impossibly hard and deathly cruel. As did the Hebrews' slavery in Egypt. As did the wandering in the wilderness. Yet for every impossible setback came a redemptive response: first, the call of Abraham, instituting God's covenant with a chosen people; then their Exodus from bondage; then their open door to the Promised Land.

But though each reversal of destiny figured significantly into our spiritual history—though each remedy served a valuable purpose to the people who experienced it—none of these heroic treatment options dealt permanently with man's chronic condition. None provided the full healing our hearts so desperately needed. They did a lot, yes, but they were only designed to do so much. And we, well . . .

We don't just need a lot. We need it all.

As Ephesians 1:23 puts it, we need "all in all."

We need all of God. We need everything.

And he, our all and everything, is Jesus.

Who, thankfully, got here right on time.

BETWEEN THE TESTAMENTS

Warning: a lot of history is about to be crammed here into a very small space. The intervening years between Malachi and Matthew seem quiet from a spiritual perspective. They were not quiet from a geopolitical perspective.

Put the emergence of the Greeks in there; put Alexander the Great in there. Sweeping west to east, he overwhelmed the Persian Empire, seizing control of their vast territory, including the area around Jerusalem, a region the Greeks renamed as Palestine. (Think of Palestine as roughly equivalent to what we've been calling Canaan or the Promised Land.) Regime change also brought Greek language and influence to this part of the world, a transformative cultural process known as Hellenism.

After the death of Alexander, Palestine switched hands a time or three among various Greek military leaders, each of which generally allowed the Jews to keep practicing their religious life without interference. But the worldly, modern, liberating allure of Hellenism soon began to fray the people's loyalties to God and each other. Eventually, these widening rifts outgrew the living rooms of private debate, spilling out into more public expressions of conflict and unrest. Seeking to put down the disturbance, Antiochus IV (ruler of Palestine in the 160s BC) lowered the Hellenistic boom. He imposed restrictions on Jewish traditions and customs, such as forbidding their reading of the Hebrew law, their observance of the Sabbath, and the circumcision of their children. (I suppose if I was given a multiple-choice test, I'd be cool with *one* of those things going away.) But he also took it to an infuriating, in-your-face next step.

PERIODS BETWEEN OLD AND NEW TESTAMENTS

The prophet Daniel had actually foretold these events centuries earlier, looking ahead to a time when enemy forces would "rise up and desecrate the temple," when an outsider would "abolish the regular sacrifice and set up the abomination of desolation" (Dan. 11:31 csb). Did he ever. Among other things, Antiochus erected an altar to Zeus in the Jewish temple and sacrificed a pig on it as a burnt offering. Don't forget that pigs were considered horribly unclean to Jews, so this was the ultimate insult.

You may or may not recognize the name of Judas Maccabeus, who led the charge to regain control of Jerusalem. He was the son of a priest and refused to give an offering to Zeus. (Haven't we all been there?) He gathered up a crew of folks and revolted. Despite all odds, they won the battle and pushed their enemies out of Jerusalem.

Have you heard of Hanukkah? Perfect. Well, now you know you can tuck that story right here too, between the two testaments of Scripture. The eight-day Feast of Lights commemorates the time when the Jews took the temple back, cleansing it and rededicating it as they became an independent nation.

But after a hundred years of back-and-forth turbulence, Palestine was again overtaken by another world empire—the Romans—the largest and most all-consuming to date. Put Julius Caesar in there; put Antony and Cleopatra in there. Also put King Herod in there, only don't think of "Herod" as being a single individual's name but rather a family designation, sort of like the Tudors or the Windsors. (Several different Herods appear in the New Testament. It's super easy to get them mixed up.)

Herod I, for starters—Herod the Great—was delegated by the Roman senate in 40 BC to serve as caretaker over Palestine. But get this: Herod's family line traced indirectly through the Edomites. Therefore, the Jews considered him particularly unfit to be ruling over their affairs. Think about why that would be the case. Ohhhh, wait . . . those two brothers and the goat hair thing.

But in an attempt to gain their allegiance, as well as impress his Roman benefactors, Herod entered into a grand building campaign, including a lavish refurbishing of the Jewish Temple (which at this point was still called Zerubbabel's Temple, dating back to Ezra and Nehemiah's day). He would call this new version Herod's Temple, and bless Zerubbabel, your glory days are over, sir.

This version of the temple—the third and last, which was destroyed for good by the Romans in AD 70—became the site of many events throughout Jesus' life and the entire New Testament era.

So, just as a reminder: the first temple was built by Solomon; the second was built by Jews who'd been released from captivity (Zarubbabel's Temple); and the third was renovated and expanded by a Roman ruler who was trying to win favor from the Israelites (Herod's Temple).

But overall, for the first time in maybe forever, a general sense of peace and order (the *Pax Romana*) settled across the world. A single empire, whose network of roads made possible the free flow of travel, commerce, and ideas from the Mediterranean to the Atlantic, now lay open to the most revolutionary idea of all. As the apostle Paul would later say, "When the fullness of time had come, God sent forth his Son" (Gal. 4:4). He sent him into a culture that provided ample room for his message to ignite a small band of impassioned followers and for the resulting wildfire to spread in all directions.

And so, "in those days a decree went out from Caesar Augustus that all the world should be registered" (Luke 2:1) . . . as if the notion just happened to come to him. But as we've seen in our study of Scripture and biblical

THE ROMAN EMPIRE AT JESUS' BIRTH

precedent, "the king's heart is a stream of water in the hand of the LORD; he turns it wherever he will" (Prov. 21:1). And the Lord was about to turn the entire tide of history toward the little town of Bethlehem.

THE GOSPEL TRUTH

All right, let's take a quick survey of what's around us as we flip past the title page in our Bible that says "The New Testament." We're now looking at Matthew, Mark, Luke, and John, officially known as the four Gospels. Each of them, written by different men, gives an account of the life of Christ. But as we saw when passing through the Old Testament books of Kings and Chronicles, each Gospel writer put together his individual biography for a specific audience and for a slightly different purpose.

MATTHEW

Matthew was a Jewish follower of Christ. And he hoped to convince his fellow Jews that this man who was killed on a cross and then rose from the dead was, indeed, the prophesied Messiah they'd been told to be watching for.

This knowledge about Matthew explains two things that are pretty evident when reading his book, even as early as its opening pages.

First, all of us know the importance of how a book begins. We know the weight a movie director places on the opening scene. Hook 'em right up front, and you've immediately got their attention. So how does Matthew start? With seventeen verses that read like a phone book. Probably not where you'd want to begin your Scripture memory program.

But in Jewish culture, ancestry is critically important. And Matthew knew how to read a room. Having been on this journey that you and I have been traveling for all these pages, how intrigued do you think a Jewish reader would be when handed "the book of the genealogy of Jesus Christ, the son of David, the son of Abraham" (Matt. 1:1)? This is not just some boring family reunion.

God had told Abraham that all the families of the earth would be blessed through him. *But how?* He'd told David that a king would sit on his throne forever. *But who?* Matthew's got your answer. From Abraham, through David, and down through their generations, this covenant family lineage produced a man named "Joseph the husband of Mary, of whom Jesus was born, who is called Christ" (v. 16).

Boom.

Matthew instantly had the Jews' attention.

Then second, he began telling the now-familiar story of how Mary, though an unmarried girl who'd never been intimate with a man, became pregnant by the miraculous intervention of the Holy Spirit. To which Matthew quickly stated, in verses 22–23, "All this took place to fulfill what the Lord had spoken by the prophet *[the prophet Isaiah]*: 'Behold, the virgin shall conceive and bear a son, and they shall call his name Immanuel' (which means, God with us)."

Prophecy fulfilled, again and again—prophecies from Isaiah, Hosea, Micah, Zechariah, Jeremiah, even from the Psalms and the mouth of their hero, David. Over and over throughout his book, Matthew presents a story from Jesus' life, then connects it to a specific Old Testament prophecy, which he spells out right there in the text, side by side. By showing how precisely Jesus fulfilled what the prophets had predicted, he makes the case that Jesus is their Messiah. Jesus is their King. Jesus came to establish not a kingdom of the earth, but the kingdom of heaven.

MARK

Mark's Gospel appears second, and his goal for writing was to tell not the Jews but the *Romans* about Jesus. And so in the action-packed, stick-to-the-facts method that the Romans loved and preferred, Mark delivered an account of Christ's life that is quick and to the point. Practical and straight ahead. "Here he is; here's what he did." Subject, verb. Period, paragraph. That's all his audience cared about. Just show them the evidence and don't waste their time.

Which is fine. That's the way God made certain people; that's why Mark's book is in the Bible. As for me though, I'm just going to be honest and tell you: that's why Mark is not my favorite of the four. His Gospel is obviously Scripture, so I ascribe to it all the authority of God's truth, same as the others. But I'm willing to say I'm glad the Lord chose to include, for the rest of us who like the juicy details, Gospel writers like . . .

LUKE

Luke was Dr. Detail. And, yes, he was actually a doctor. Which, I suppose, made him naturally more inquisitive and interested in the various shades of expression that colored each happening of Jesus he described. I mean, in Mark's case, I can imagine his classmates voting him "Most Likely to Be Efficient." He was probably a really swell guy. But Luke, I guess, thought a few extra observations were always worth the ink and paper costs. And I like that quality about him and his writing style.

But let's also compare Luke to Matthew. In the same way that Matthew was a Jewish believer speaking to Jews, Luke was a native Greek speaking to Gentiles. He wrote to people who didn't possess a childhood grasp of the Hebrew Scriptures, who didn't know to be on the lookout for a king who would rule on David's throne. Luke's objective was to show his worldly readers a man who was unlike any other, a Jewish man who had a message for Gentiles as well.

That's why when Luke made the decision to include a more robust record of Jesus' genealogy, he didn't stop at Abraham, once he got that deep into the family tree. He kept working backward—past Shem and Noah, past Methuselah and Enoch, all the way back to "the son of Enos, the son of Seth, the son of Adam, the son of God" (Luke 3:38). Whereas Matthew mainly wanted to unmask Jesus' identity as the Jewish Messiah, Luke wanted to reveal Jesus' connection to the whole human race. The Jews, of course, already knew that Abraham linked back up to Adam, but the Greeks didn't. So, Luke crafted the genealogy with them in mind.

Matthew, Mark, Luke: these three books of the Bible are known as the Synoptic Gospels, meaning they provide a collective *synopsis* of Jesus' life and ministry. In normal people terms, this means they're each a big summary of where this Jesus guy came from and what he did with his time. I've told you about the subtle differences between these books, and yet when you're reading any one of them, you'll notice a lot of commonality in what they cover. The distinction is more in nuance and vantage points, not so much new material. The same is *not* the case, however, with . . .

JOHN

John also was a Jew, like Matthew. But John wrote for everyone: Jew or Gentile; Roman or Greek. He wrote more thematically. He wrote more poetically. He played with symbolism and painted his account of Jesus with deep dimensions, using concepts of light and darkness, day and night, water and fire, and so on. He chose events from

Jesus' life that the other Gospel writers chose not to feature
for the most part.

John just seemed more interested not only in encouraging others' belief—in getting people to acknowledge Jesus
as God's Messiah, as God's Son—but in wanting them to
go deeper with Jesus, to find through him a whole new
dimension of life. He wanted them not just to be informed,
but to reflect.

From the first syllables on the first page, you can
instantly tell the difference in his writing style. "In the
beginning was the Word, and the Word was with God,
and the Word was God" (John 1:1). Notice how he went
back even further than the days of Adam. He took Jesus'
backstory to a time before Creation even began. "In the
beginning."

And the beauty of John's language about Jesus just
keeps on flowing:

> He came to his own, and his own people did
> not receive him. But to all who did receive
> him, who believed in his name, he gave the
> right to become children of God, who were
> born, not of blood nor of the will of the flesh
> nor of the will of man, but of God.
>
> And the Word became flesh and dwelt
> among us, and we have seen his glory, glory
> as of the only Son from the Father, full of
> grace and truth. (John 1:11–14)

I still get goose bumps.

So nothing personal, Mark, but my favorite is John,
who often just lets Jesus talk for long red-letter passages
at a time. (You know what I mean by "red letters," right?
Many Bibles use red-colored type for the words Jesus said.)
John gives Jesus lots of this red-lettered green space for
declaring what he came to Earth to do, how he wants us

to "abide" in him like branches on a vine (John 15:4), how we can find in him the one thing we're all seeking, which nothing and no one else can ever give us: "I came that they may have life and have it abundantly" (John 10:10).

Those are your four *Gospels* (the Greek word for "good news").

Matthew, Mark, Luke, and John.

This may come as a surprise to you, if you've pictured all four of these folks wandering around with Jesus. That's not exactly true. Matthew and John did. They were disciples who walked with Jesus. Mark, though, was not in Jesus' traveling party. It's highly likely, based on the style of writing in his book, that Mark was reporting the testimony Peter gave him. (We'll meet Peter later.) Finally, Dr. Luke. It's entirely possible that Luke never even *met* Jesus, but he extensively interviewed eyewitnesses and meticulously put his book together based on their testimonies.

I wish I could ask you if you were surprised. *I was.* I had always pictured them as a crew.

To be extra clear, though—and please don't feel embarrassed if you didn't really know this—Matthew, Mark, Luke, and John are not like movie sequels: Part I, Part II, Part III, Part IV. *The Jesus Story in Four Acts.* Instead, they are independent biographies. They each begin at an early moment in Jesus' life (or, as we've seen with John, *before* his earthly life) and they take us through his crucifixion, his resurrection, and beyond.

Now in between these general bookends, the Gospel writers chose different events and sayings of Jesus to report on and highlight.

In certain cases, for instance, a single Gospel will be the only place where a particular story is told (like, say, Luke's inclusion of the story about the "wee little man" Zacchaeus from the well-known children's song).

In other places, two or as many as three of the writers will relate the same story, though perhaps with slightly different details or focus (such as Jesus' walking on the water, found in Matthew 14, Mark 6, and John 6).

Every so often, the same miracle or occurrence will show up in all four books. (One example is Jesus' feeding of the five thousand.)

Here's what I'm saying: no single Gospel is the whole story, mainly because no single book about Jesus' life could ever possibly be the whole story. John famously said there were so many things Jesus said and did that "were every one of them to be written, I suppose that the world itself could not contain the books that would be written" (John 21:25).

Touché.

So, while each of the Gospels by itself can certainly be enjoyed and learned from, the best way to get the broadest feel for everything they tell us about the life of Jesus is by blending them. It's like when somebody does a documentary about the life of a public figure. They don't interview only *one* person, then frame the whole picture around that. Instead, they piece together insights and remembrances from a whole bunch of people who were close to this man or woman.

It's in the synthesizing of their various reflections that the whole person develops. They may even be talking about a single event which every one of them witnessed or heard about, but each person's viewpoint provides a somewhat different perspective on it. We don't want to hear about it from only a single, unison voice. We want it told to us in harmony.

The reason I use this specific term—*harmony*—is not because of how much I love singing songs about Jesus. Actually, singing to Jesus is probably not my best offering of praise to God or to anyone who might be near me. Fun fact: I have a recurring nightmare that I'm on a stage and everyone is waiting for me to sing. I also have recurring dreams that I'm lost on a campus and I know I'm supposed to get to my class because I haven't been there all semester. Or the one where my teeth shatter. Too much? My bad.

There's a type of Bible reference that would be super helpful if you're trying to get hold of these kinds of details, and it's called a *Harmony of the Gospels.*

There are actually several foundational Bible study books that are invaluable to have on your bookshelf. A *Bible Dictionary,* for one, is an alphabetical guide to the people, places, and things that appear in Scripture, complete with instructive articles and definitions. A *Bible Handbook* is more of a book-by-book survey, containing brief summaries of what's inside each chapter. Both of these are great, along with such things as a good *Study Bible,* which is just like a regular Bible, only a lot fatter because it includes a lot of insightful notes along the bottom of each page. *Commentaries* go even deeper, usually dedicating an entire volume to the study of one particular book of the Bible.

But a *Harmony of the Gospels* . . . I use mine all the time. It takes the entire text of all four Gospels and presents it in parallel columns: sometimes one, sometimes two, sometimes three, sometimes four, depending on how many writers wove that event into their narrative. You end up with a side-by-side comparison of all four books, plus you can trace the entire life of Jesus in chronological, time line order. It *harmonizes* the full quartet of Gospels. All in one.

Very cool.

And since I bet you're going to be getting your own copy pretty soon, you don't need *me* to try recreating that experience for you here. But let's at least hit the high spots of what we know about Jesus' life from putting all the Gospels together.

JESUS' ADVANCE MAN

Isaiah, seven centuries before Jesus arrived on the scene, spoke of a future prophet who would come as his forerunner: "A voice cries: 'In the wilderness prepare the way of the LORD; make straight in the desert a highway for our God'" (Isa. 40:3). Then in Matthew 3, we're finally able to put a face with that voice. John the Baptist, it says, came "preaching in the wilderness of Judea," telling people to "repent, for the kingdom of heaven is at hand." And to be sure there was no mistake as to John's true identity, Matthew just blurted out, "This is he who was spoken of by the prophet Isaiah" (Matt. 3:1–3).

Malachi, too, had quoted God as saying, "Behold, I will send you Elijah the prophet before the great and awesome day of the LORD comes" (Mal. 4:5). We haven't talked about Elijah in this book, but he played a significant prophetic role during the reign of Israel's King Ahab, one of the many wicked rulers of the Northern Kingdom. (If you've never heard of Ahab, you've most likely heard of his even more wicked queen, Jezebel. Do you remember me mentioning earlier how she was thrown off a balcony and killed by dogs?) Elijah was a hairy, rugged, crusty kind of dude whose life spanned the end of 1 Kings and the opening chapters of 2 Kings. He was the type of guy who'd say anything to anybody if God told him to say it. And as we know too well, people don't always like the sound of the truth.

John the Baptist was that same type of person—an Elijah kind of person—a man who didn't exactly prioritize personal hygiene. Jesus said of him, "All the Prophets and the Law prophesied until John," that "he is Elijah who is to come" (Matt. 11:13–14). Again, prophecy in motion.

But let's drop John more precisely into the time line, shortly before the birth of Christ. Just after Mary was told that she was carrying the Son of God (cue awkward dinner with Joseph), the angel told her that her barren, older cousin Elizabeth was pregnant. She was pregnant with John. Mary traveled up to see her, and when she entered the room, the baby in Elizabeth's belly jumped in response to the presence of Jesus in Mary's womb.

If John were on a dating app, he'd have had one of the most interesting Tinder profiles in the history of the world. He ate locusts and honey. He wore a garment of camel hair. He was essentially a wild man who lived in the desert for his entire life and then reappeared when Jesus came on the scene.

But did you skip past the stuff I mentioned at the top of this section? About Isaiah and Malachi? I hope not, but I don't mind saying it again. Hundreds of years before John came, God used the prophets to tell his people that someone like John was coming. It wasn't just a coincidence. I guess that's what I want to make sure you're understanding. Can you pull back the lens and think about the odds of all of this? Everything was falling into place exactly how God said it would. Seamlessly. And now it would continue.

JESUS' ADVENT

Jesus, the Christ, is the One who fulfilled all prophecy given to us in the Old Testament, starting before he even took a breath.

According to the prophets, Jesus was to be born in Bethlehem. But that's not where Mary and Joseph were living at the time. The only reason they went to Bethlehem was because a census was being conducted there, and everyone had to go to their hometown in order to be registered.

While they were there, Mary went into labor. Jesus was born—probably not in a manger, although the Bible does say they *laid* him in a manger. Some say he was likely born in a cave. Others say he was possibly born on the lowest floor of an inn—the open-air basement with dirt floors where the livestock and supplies were kept. That's why a manger may have been there. Either way, he was not born into luxury the way you'd expect for the King of the universe!

But I'm going to take a quick detour here so you and I can have a heart-to-heart. I don't know how many nativity sets you own or how much you paid for them, but I'm asking you not to hate me by the end of this section. I just need to report on what actually happened, and it's a wee bit problematic if you've based your understanding of Jesus' birth on a couple of Christmas carols. I'll add to this detour by telling you that our family has never made it a single year without at least two legs falling off our nativity animals. It's usually the goats.

Let's start with this: not only was Jesus not born on December 25, he wasn't even born in winter.

Also, the wise men didn't come to meet Jesus until he was a toddler, and it wasn't in Bethlehem. I have a friend, a pastor, who sets the wise men on the other side of the room from the nativity set. Cracks me up, but it's accurate.

And there weren't just three. There were likely hundreds! But it's hard to stuff that many people in Styrofoam. The reason tradition has left us with three is because Scripture says they brought him three gifts; it doesn't say there were three wise men.

Now that we've got that out of the way, let's meet the folks who met Jesus first. Were they kings? Rich people? Wait, was it a rabbi?

Actually, it was—drumroll!—shepherds.

Yes, *shepherds*, who were considered unclean and untrustworthy. They were outcasts whose testimony wasn't even allowable as public record because the people wouldn't accept it. And yet the first eyes to look into the eyes of the

Savior of the world were on the faces of people who were despised.

| Matthew (Jews) |
| Mark (Roman Gentiles) |
| Luke (Greek Gentiles) |
| John (Jews and Gentiles) |

GOSPEL WRITERS: PRIMARY AUDIENCES

Interesting speculation: some scholars and historians believe these particular shepherds were in charge of tending to very special lambs. Do you remember the Day of Atonement, where the high priest made an offering? Well, he couldn't just offer any lamb. It had to be a spotless, perfect lamb. It's possible the first people outside of Mary and Joseph who saw the living Christ were shepherds raising perfect lambs for sacrifice.

It must have been a pretty huge task to take care of these unblemished lambs. What pressure to keep them safe and protected. Which is likely why, as soon as they were born, the shepherds wrapped them in swaddling cloth—*a beautiful, spotless lamb, swaddled and raised to be a perfect offering.*

Nothing is by chance. This is the beautiful part of Scripture. You can never get to the end of it. There's always more to learn, to dig into, to piece together.

Isn't that beautiful?

Now from here, we don't know much about Jesus' childhood, other than that he "grew in wisdom and in stature and in favor with God and man" (Luke 2:52 NIV). The only other window that shines any light on Jesus as a boy comes from the one time where Mary lost him for a couple of days, which blesses me as a mother.

I definitely lost one of my twins in a bookstore once. While holding the other on my hip, I started darting around, panicked. I looked up and saw (I kid you not) Tim McGraw standing there, because, Nashville. He instantly started looking around with me, and it was obvious to him that he'd found her, mostly because both of my kids' heads looked exactly the same. (Thank you, Tim. Where were you when I lost Kate at Disney World and found her in the "terrible parents" room coloring a picture of Goofy and acting like everything was awesome?) Cool. Next up for me is a parenting book.

Anyway, Mary really did lose Jesus, on their way back home from Jerusalem after going there for Passover. They'd walked all day, figuring he was probably just somewhere with his cousins or friends, before Mary had her "KEVIN!" moment. Not until after *three days* of searching did they find him back at the temple, where they'd all been together the last time they'd seen him. There they found him teaching all the rabbis, who were amazed by his knowledge. A kid teaching rabbis! He then held up a picture of Minnie Mouse that he'd colored, and don't you KNOW he stayed in the lines! Still, Mary was angry at him for not keeping up with the pack of people who'd been heading home, and for worrying her to death. Oddly enough, though, he asked her why she'd been looking for him: "Did you not know that I must be in my Father's house?" (Luke 2:49).

Those words weren't sarcastic. They were an indication that the tide was changing. No longer would Jesus simply be a normal twelve-year-old boy. His ministry was beginning, and he wanted to make clear that the temple was more of a home to him than Mary's house. Jesus knew who he was. He knew what he'd been set on this earth to do.

This was the day she'd always known would come, and yet it didn't change the gravity of the moment. He was speaking to his mother who remembered him as a three-year-old, falling while trying to run to the neighbor's house; as a six-year-old who beamed from ear to ear when he got to go to work with his dad and learn the family trade; as an eight-year-old who didn't really like soup very much when he sat at the lunch table of his synagogue school; as a ten-year-old who didn't need bedtime stories anymore.

Now he was twelve. And in some sense, he was saying goodbye.

Yes, he was her son.

But he was also the Son of God.

And in about twenty years, he would formally be introduced to the world by the cousin who liked long walks on the beach and locust salad.

> He [John] saw Jesus coming toward him,
> and said, "Behold, the Lamb of God, who
> takes away the sin of the world!" (John 1:29)

Even though John and Jesus were related, we'd be speculating to guess if they knew each other growing up. Even if so, they apparently hadn't seen one another in a long time because John, in remarking about how he'd spotted Jesus among the crowd that day, said he didn't really know him, except that this Man was the reason he'd camped out at the river to baptize people, "that he might be revealed to Israel" (John 1:31).

So while Jesus had been orbiting in relative obscurity in his hometown of Nazareth—a backwards, backwoods village a good sixty miles north of Jerusalem, in a region of Palestine known as Galilee—this moment at the Jordan marked the beginning of his active ministry. He who had lived in private perfection for thirty years had been preparing a literal eternity for this public day. Matthew, Mark, and Luke each tell the story of Jesus walking out into the river where John waited with heart beating rapidly, saying, "I need to be baptized by you, and do you come to me?" (Matt. 3:14).

But this was how it was meant to be. And it could hardly have happened with more meaning.

> When Jesus was baptized, immediately he went up from the water, and behold, the heavens were opened to him, and he saw the Spirit of God descending like a dove and coming to rest on him; and behold, a voice from heaven said, "This is my beloved Son, with whom I am well pleased." (Matt. 3:16–17)

It was starting. And there'd be no looking back.

JESUS' ADVENTURES

Right after Jesus was baptized, "the Spirit immediately drove him out into the wilderness" to be "tempted by Satan" (Mark 1:12–13).

Okay then. Awesome thing to walk into, first day on the job.

But in God's defense, this early episode sure is instructive. It becomes a riveting, real-life example for us, showing us how to fight back against our enemy when he tries to use the same tactics against *us*. It also echoes back to the garden of Eden—Jesus succeeding in all the places of Satan's temptation where Adam and Eve failed, though Satan never misses an opportunity to go for the jugular. *You have everything you've ever wanted. You can pull off everything you came here to do. You can be the King of the world in a position of power and knowledge and might, if you do it my way.* Yet where Adam and Eve failed to trust God's word to them and fell for the enemy's scheme, Jesus didn't.

He used that Word as an offensive weapon. He consistently rebuked Satan with Scripture, until the devil finally just gave up and left, waiting for a more "opportune time" (Luke 4:13). This particular plan obviously wasn't working.

After his trial in the desert (you'll never imagine how many days it lasted—yep, forty), he called twelve men to form his core group of disciples:

- Simon (fisherman, later called Peter)
- Andrew (fisherman, Peter's brother)
- James (fisherman, brother of John)
- John (fisherman, Gospel writer)
- Philip (told Nathanael about Jesus in John 1)
- Bartholomew (may actually be Nathanael)
- Thomas (doubting Thomas)
- Matthew (tax collector/Gospel writer)
- James (different James: son of Alphaeus)
- Thaddeus (also known as Judas)
- Simon (different Simon: the Zealot)
- Judas Iscariot (but why, Jesus? Urggh!)

He gave this group of twelve the authority to perform miracles, like healing people's illnesses and casting out demons. Then, as Mark said, he sent them out in pairs. But Matthew was quick to add one further detail. He shared the part of their marching orders where Jesus told them to go first "to the lost sheep of the house of Israel" (Matt. 10:6). *To Israel,* God's beloved people. Jesus came with a message to the Jews that sounded a whole lot like what the Lord had been saying to them for centuries through Moses, through Samuel, through the prophets, and others—an urgent appeal to repent and return to him, to follow the life-giving leadership of their loving King.

But they wouldn't. He knew they wouldn't. Yet it was important that he start there. To start with *them*. To show he had not abandoned Israel. To show he was bound to them not just by covenant, not just by chromosomes, but by heart. Remember how the prophets showed God's desire to clean house within his own people first? Jesus, as the ultimate prophet—and as *God*, mind you—was doing the same.

And so, over and over throughout the Gospels, we see him coming face-to-face with the members of the Jewish leadership, only to be told they wanted nothing to do with either him or his so-called "kingdom of heaven."

Maybe you've heard of some of these guys, the religious leaders of Israel. Want to know more about them? Hope you said yes, because you're stuck with me. We're friends now.

Pharisees. They stood on the ultraconservative plank of the Jewish platform. When you hear the term "Pharisee" in the New Testament, think *law, law, law*. They were sticklers not only for observance of the law but for their own strict, added-on interpretations of it. This means they added a bunch of their own made-up traditions to God's law, forcing the Jewish people to obey *both*. Which was a lot. The Pharisees ran the synagogues and exercised control over the people's religious life, even though "holier than thou" hypocrisy was rampant among them. Nobody's perfect. Just don't tell that to a Pharisee.

Sadducees. Think of Sadducees as the liberals. At least in a relative sense. They adhered to the law, but they were the wealthier, more cultured class who'd been Hellenized into becoming progressives. So, they rejected some of the traditional Jewish teachings, particularly the belief in life after death—resurrection—and the idea that people receive reward or punishment beyond one's earthly existence.

They deemed Jesus a threat to their aristocratic position and status.

Pharisees and Sadducees were the main two Jewish parties of the day. They were the ones who put up the most resistance to Jesus, who considered him a blasphemous troublemaker. But the Gospels refer to another couple of groups who opposed and challenged Jesus.

Scribes were Jewish lawyers, legal experts on the Mosaic law. They thought Jesus was taking dangerous liberties with God's Word (which is funny because he *was* "the Word").

The Sanhedrin was a seventy-one member Jewish council presided over by the high priest. Like in today's forms of governments, the Sanhedrin was comprised of members from dueling parties, mostly Pharisees and Sadducees, but also a few other minority voices.

Taken together, these haughty, power-protecting people represented the official, party-line rejection of Jesus' claims that he was the Son of God. To them, he wasn't the way, the truth, and the life; he was simply a problem.

And they had ways of dealing with a problem.

But to the outcast and rejected, to the poor and needy, to the struggling simple classes of both Jewish and Gentile culture, Jesus was a fascinating, likable, powerful figure who captivated their lost sense of hope and drew them toward his attractive authenticity.

He taught them. The Sermon on the Mount is the most lengthy example of his teaching, covering the entirety of Matthew 5–7 and found in condensed form inside Luke 6. But the Gospels frequently refer to people flocking to hear his teaching. Sometimes they traveled so far and stayed so long that they forgot they hadn't eaten. That's why on one occasion he ended up needing to feed five thousand of them with a few pieces of bread and some fish sticks. Have you heard that story?

He taught them in parables. One of the things that made his teaching so effective with the common people was that he often taught in stories. His many parables used simple analogies to present deep, groundbreaking truth. They conveyed in memorable fashion "the secrets of the kingdom of heaven" (Matt. 13:11). That's why we still remember them so vividly—the Prodigal Son, the Good Samaritan, the tiny mustard seed that grows to become the largest of plants.

He performed miracles for them. To prove he was the Son of God and to point to the type of kingdom that was to come, he openly displayed his power over disease, over blindness, over the weather, over demonic activity. Life in the resurrection wouldn't have all that stuff—all these results of the Fall that plague humanity today—and he wanted to give snapshots of what that life to come would actually be like. He wanted to remind people of what life is supposed to look like without the ravages of sin and suffering and death—life that really could be theirs one day in the new heavens and the new earth if they believed in him. So, he loved and served and cared and ministered. He spent much time with his Father in prayer, much time with his disciples as their mentor, and much time with the masses, yet always found time to deal with people on a personal, fully engaged basis.

He obeyed God perfectly. In all his ministry, in all his days from his birth, Jesus obeyed the will of the Father at every turn, in every moment. Can you imagine? We all fall short of perfection, but Jesus didn't. He showed the world what a sinless human looked like. He kept the law and all of God's standards for righteousness every second of every day, and he did it with right motives too. He did everything right, and *for all the right reasons*. He was accumulating a righteous, perfect record, inside and out. No black marks. No points docked. No moment of failure or even being off the mark by a centimeter. Every expectation of God, satisfied. Everything. Perfectly.

That's what Jesus did. That's who Jesus was (and is). That's the story the Gospels tell, throughout chapter after chapter of their individual narratives. Jesus was born. Jesus grew. Jesus came to John at the Jordan River, which launched his three-year ministry of teaching, healing, and miracle-working. Jesus came to the earth so we could hear the Word for ourselves, spoken in language we could understand, for anyone who really *wants* to understand.

But as amazing as those years were—and I mean *truly* amazing!—they were funneling toward events that made all history pale in comparison.

The events of a single week.

Chapter 12

LIKE HE ALWAYS SAID HE WOULD
Cross and Resurrection

 The writers of the four Gospels, as we've seen, skipped around as to which events they chose to cover from Jesus' birth story and the first three years of his public ministry. But by the time he started heading toward Jerusalem for his final Passover, all hands were on deck. Why? Because this week was the reason Jesus had a ministry to begin with. Everything Jesus did was in preparation for THIS WEEK. It's why people call it Holy Week (Palm Sunday to Easter Sunday), and give special attention to it with rituals like fasting, prayer, and over-the-top worship services. This was the most important, most sacred week in the history of the world.

(I know what you're thinking—*but why, oh, why do people celebrate with all the palm branches? Is it like a reverse, tropical version of Christmas trees?* I promise we'll get there.)

If you want to locate all the recorded events that led up to his triumphant entry into the city, through his crucifixion, to his resurrection, and beyond, look for them in the following chapters:

- Matthew 21–28
- Mark 11–16
- Luke 19–24
- John 12–21

So just doing the math here, seeing where these foundational moments from the story of Christianity appear, they cover about the back third or so of each Gospel. A little less of that percentage in Matthew, a lot more in John. (Oh, John, what would we do without you?)

Yet Jesus had been prepping his disciples far in advance of these events. He had told them he would be rejected by the Jewish leadership, that he would suffer, that he would be killed—and after that, he would rise again. He said it *plainly,* the Bible says. Not just plainly, but often. Time and again, Jesus would take them off by themselves and say, in so many words, "Listen, guys, here's what's about to happen." It's sort of how you'd say it to a three-year-old, you know, like, "We're stopping in ten minutes to use the bathroom. If anybody needs to go, you'll need to do it then, because we won't be stopping again for at least another hour. *Does everybody understand?"*

I mean, look at this. When Jesus and the Twelve were walking toward Jerusalem this week, where he knew it was all going down, he said to them, "See, we are going up to Jerusalem" (Mark 10:33). Can't you just hear the "Are you paying attention!" in his voice? Like he's cupping a little kid's face in his hands, and saying, "I need you to look me in the eye, okay? I need to be sure you hear what I'm saying to you." He again told them the same thing, making the same predictions, how the people would mock him and beat him and spit on him and kill him. And after three days he would rise.

Was he trying to keep any of this a secret from his disciples? No.

But did they understand him? No.

The only word of it they seemed to hear, whenever he brought it up, was that he would be "killed." And it distressed them to no end to hear him talking that way. It's like how we've all felt whenever our parents would try speaking with us about their will or their funeral arrangements. You just don't want to discuss it. You don't want to think about it. *Can we please talk about something else?*

Peter, the most headstrong of the disciples, just finally had enough of it. He took Jesus to the side one day and told him to stop saying such awful things. Matthew described the tone of Peter's words as a rebuke, stunned by how brazenly Peter spoke to their leader. Yet Jesus rocked him backward with the force of his reaction: "Get behind me, Satan! You are a hindrance to me. For you are not setting your mind on the things of God, but on the things of man" (Matt. 16:22–23). Wow, that's not a gentle statement.

Because ironically enough, even in sounding like he was defending him, Peter was actually working against him. And Jesus already had more than enough people working against him.

Although, to tell you the truth, everything was going exactly according to plan, every last inch and stitch of it.

Jesus' suffering and death—all of it—was all in God's plan.

WEEKLY READER

Some of Jesus' most well-known sayings and actions happened right here during this week, mere days before he was arrested, tried, and killed.

Six days before Passover, the Bible says they came to Bethany, about two miles outside Jerusalem, "where Lazarus was, whom Jesus had raised from the dead" (John 12:1). I'd warned you from the start we wouldn't be able to land on every event from Scripture in this book, but I'm sorry now we had to blow past this one: the resurrection of Jesus' friend Lazarus.

"Jesus wept" that day—shortest verse in the Bible (John 11:35)—standing outside his friend's sealed-up tomb. But when Jesus instructed the stone to be removed from the tomb and then called out to him, telling him to come out of his grave, Lazarus emerged resurrected. Big-time miracle.

Word of Jesus' miracles never failed to get around. But word of someone being RAISED FROM THE DEAD . . . that *really* got around. A walking, talking Lazarus was living proof that Jesus was a lot more than just a good communicator. He was nothing less than God in flesh—"the resurrection and the life" (John 11:25)—which many people were beginning to see and believe. *Um, you guys, you know how people always die at some point? This guy can just speak a word and, you know, basically reverse that.*

One interesting tidbit here: Jesus waited four days after Lazarus died before he came back, which must have seemed really cruel. It was very deliberate on his part, though. People at that time thought the spirit of a person could hover around him for three days and at any point bring him back to life. Jesus waited until the fourth day to ensure that everyone knew Lazarus was actually dead.

Anyway, back to the six days before Passover. Lazarus, as well as his two sisters (Mary and Martha), were true believers. And on this evening in Bethany, with Jesus on his way to Jerusalem, Mary proved her devotion to him by unsealing a container of expensive perfume and pouring it out on his feet, toweling up the overage with her own hair. Such a tender, beautiful expression of worship.

We've all been fascinated by this story whenever we've heard it or read it. It grips us. It challenges us. Judas, however, who served as treasurer for the disciples, complained of all the waste that Mary's act represented. He wasn't just focused on the money; he was testing Jesus to see if *he* would agree that it was a waste.

The next day, Jesus went on into Jerusalem. Again, it was Passover week. (Do you remember what Passover is? Do you remember the day when hyssop branches, soaked with blood, had rescued God's people in Egypt?

Do you remember the day when death came for the first-borns, but anyone with blood swiped on their house was "passed over," avoiding death?) Though anyone else with Jesus' claims of divine authority might have showed up on horseback, he rode into town atop a common donkey. Still, he was greeted by chants of "Hosanna! Blessed is he who comes in the name of the Lord" (John 12:13), shouted by people who carpeted his path with palm branches.

Matthew, of course, read prophetic fulfillment into the moment, from back where Zechariah had said, "Behold, your king is coming to you, humble, and mounted on a donkey, and on a colt, the foal of a beast of burden" (Matt. 21:5). Do you understand how ridiculous it would be to think all of this just "happened"? See how it matches up with all the prophecy given hundreds of years prior?

Anyway, Jesus' entrance into town is known as the Triumphal Entry, and guess how we commemorate it today? Well, let's think. The people were throwing palm leaves down in front of him—palm leaves being an ancient symbol of victory. So, yep, there you go: Palm Sunday. Told you we'd get there!

But not all was celebration.

When he observed the amount of trading and transacting that was being conducted in and around the temple area—the cheating and the shortchanging—he raged across the grounds, upending the merchants' tables, driving them off the property with a handmade whip. "Is it not written," he said as he went, "'My house shall be called a house of prayer for all the nations'? But you have made it a den of robbers" (Mark 11:17).

This is what you might call "forcing the issue." His enemies were not pleased with such a display of anger.

The next day, he returned to the scene. Simply his presence, he knew, made him a lightning rod. And they couldn't help themselves from taking the bait. They peppered him with questions, seeking to trap him in some kind of doctrinal error. But Jesus answered their every question so skillfully, so expertly, that they didn't really know how to respond—and keep from looking extra two-faced.

He told parables. He predicted the future, from the fall of Jerusalem and the destruction of the temple to the final judgment itself. He also called out the scribes and Pharisees in blistering detail for their numerous examples of hypocrisy. (Try reading Matthew 23 sometime, and ask yourself why people insist on thinking of Jesus as nothing but a gentle teacher.) Catching sight of a widow dropping two measly coins into the collection box, he used her humble imagery as a contrast to their pride, greed, and pretension: "Truly, I tell you, this poor widow has put in more than all of them. For they contributed out of their abundance, but she out of her poverty put in all she had to live on" (Luke 21:3–4).

These harsh (but true!) accusations should sound strikingly familiar. Jesus, the ultimate prophet, was on full display, calling God's people out on their deception, oppression, and hypocrisy. But remember, this Jesus wasn't an ordinary prophet simply carrying God's word. This was God showing up in the flesh, and calling them out *himself*, face-to-face. And yet they still stubbornly disbelieved. Even with God in their midst.

ANATOMY OF A MURDER

The people who'd been plotting Jesus' capture were too political just to come out and declare their true colors. Perhaps they hadn't anticipated the cheering reception that he got on his arrival in Jerusalem. It had thrown their plans off schedule. For even though the religious leaders had set aside their differences with one another in order to plot how to arrest him (hopefully, to kill him), they now found they'd lost control of the timing. They didn't want to create too big of a stir and get people noticing what they were doing.

Working around our hypocrisy can be so inconvenient sometimes.

I mean, they felt pressure to maintain their Passover customs. They knew they needed to look the part. Make the appearances. Complete the steps. But the effort required in looking pious and presentable was seriously getting in the way of their assassination conspiracy. Funny how, in trying to observe every jot and tittle of the law, they somehow failed to recognize that this Jesus—the object of their murderous scorn and contempt—was himself the total fulfillment of the law.

Not funny. Pathetic.

Pathological.

Yet God was the One who actually remained in full control of these events, even while his enemies worked and reworked their contingency plans. This is the part I find impossible to fathom, how Isaiah had said, "It was the will of the LORD to crush him" and "put him to grief" (Isa. 53:10). God even served up the bagman for them, a person more suitable to their scheme than anybody they could've concocted on their own. Judas, one of Jesus' own followers, offered to give them real-time updates on his whereabouts.

What an elegant, organic solution.

An informant operating from the inside.

And to think, Jesus knew it all along. As far back as John 6, he'd already said to his tight-knit group of followers, "Did I not choose you, the twelve? And yet one of you is a devil" (v. 70).

But before they could have him—or, to say it more biblically, before he would willingly *give* himself to them—he backed off and pulled away from them. He wanted one last day with the small cluster of men who'd been beside him from the start. To read the fullest version of what he said to them during that Thursday interaction, spend some time one of these days in John 13–17, which takes you from the touching moment where he knelt down and washed their feet to the fearless moment where he knelt down and prayed for their protection. For *their* protection, not his own . . . because Judas Iscariot, that scoundrel, would be right there around the table as they were celebrating Passover. He would know Jesus' location and movements. He could tip off his employers with firsthand intel, showing them precisely how and when to apprehend their prey with the least fuss and visibility.

I wonder what Judas was acting like. He must have been avoiding eye contact and trying to calm his racing heart. These had been his traveling companions for years, and the moment was only a few hours away—the moment when he would betray the Son of Man.

During this Passover, Christ was foreshadowing what we all know to be true on this side of the resurrection.

The bread he tore wasn't just any bread.

It represented the tearing of his own flesh, his own body.

The wine he poured wasn't just any wine.

It represented the pouring out of his blood—*his OWN blood!*

You'll recognize this moment as being the first observance of what the church now calls Communion or the Lord's Supper. The reason we keep doing it, the Bible says, is to keep remembering—to never forget—what Jesus did for us.

But don't miss the clinching line that Jesus spoke at the original Communion gathering: "Behold, the hand of him who betrays me is with me on the table" (Luke 22:21).

Who, me? Judas piped up.

"You have said so," Jesus answered (Matt. 26:25).

And with that, Judas slipped into the night, leaving behind him the man he'd eaten meals with, laughed with, slept near, teased, and applauded for three years—the face of a man he'd watched perform miracles and welcome children into his arms.

The thing is, it's easy just to say, "Judas the traitor," without digging down another few layers, because they were truly friends. Think about that for a second. Think about the fact that all these men knew each other. They knew whose hair stood straight up in the morning and which ones couldn't be trusted to cook. They knew who was the biggest heartthrob, and they missed no opportunity to point out gawking women. They knew who snored and who had a hard childhood. They crossed miles in step with one another, always as a pack.

Jesus was God, yes. But he was also a man. He was part of a group. And Judas, his confidante, was about to betray him.

TERROR AT TWILIGHT

It was late now. Late Thursday night.

Judas had left on his treasonous errand; Jesus was left to be troubled by the heaviest burden any man could ever know. He and the remainder of his disciples departed to a garden just outside the walls of the city, where he asked his inner circle—Peter, James, and John—to step even deeper into his sorrow.

He asked them to sit nearby while he went over to pray: "Remain here, and watch with me" (Matt. 26:38). But they couldn't seem to sense the real danger he was in. They couldn't discern the gravity of the moment. They didn't share the intensity of Jesus' need for praying. Instead, they fell asleep, leaving him alone with his Father. Alone in his hour of deepest anguish.

You know the prayer, probably by heart: "If it be possible," he asked, "let this cup pass from me" (Matt. 26:39)—this entire ordeal of not only physical suffering (dying on behalf of a rebellious world) but also the relational cost of being separated from the Father for the first time in his existence. Sin would get credited to his flawless account, and the Father can't be in fellowship with sin. For a short while, Jesus would need to take on the felt experience of relational separation from his Father, the same experience that we are all born into. He'd have to take on not only our sin but also our *shame* before his Father. Something he'd never experienced before. And he couldn't bear the thought.

"Nevertheless, not as I will, but as you will" (v. 39). The Father's silence confirmed what Jesus already knew, what he'd known and actually chosen for himself from before the foundation of the world. The cup would not pass.

At some point that evening, Judas and his handlers arrived, armed with weapons and with anger. He had said to his coconspirators, "The one I will kiss is the man; seize him" (v. 48). So, stepping out from the brutish mob, Judas drew near to Jesus. Jesus looked him dead in the eye and said, "Friend, do what you came to do" (v. 50).

Total chaos ensued, and the end result was Jesus being dragged out of the garden and brought to the home of a retired high priest named Annas. The high priesthood by this time in Jewish history functioned more as a political office than a pastoral one, meaning this was no prayer service; it was a highly orchestrated inquisition. Annas then sent him, tied up, to his son-in-law Caiaphas, the current high priest, for another round of hard questioning.

It was during these ominous overnight proceedings, outside in the courtyard after the rest of Jesus' disciples had run away in fear, that Peter denied three times he even knew who Jesus was. Yet all the time on the inside—inside that mockery of a courtroom—"who Jesus was" was the only thing anybody wanted to talk about. People blurted out lies, shouted fabricated stories, and tried to force a confession out of him. If they could get him to commit outright blasphemy, they could have him put to death.

Yet Jesus, as Isaiah had prophesied, didn't say a word: "Like a lamb led to the slaughter and like a sheep silent before her shearers, he did not open his mouth" (Isa. 53:7 CSB). Which only infuriated them further.

"Have you no answer to make?" the high priest demanded. *I order you!*—you can almost hear his fist slamming down hard as he barked out the word—"I adjure you by the living God, tell us if you are the Christ" (Matt. 26:62–63).

Jesus' answer, classic in its indirectness, was exactly what he'd said to Judas only a few hours earlier. "You have said so," he replied. Then he tagged on something wild: "But I tell you, from now on you will see the Son of Man seated at the right hand of Power and coming on the clouds of heaven" (v. 64). It was a reference to Daniel 7:13, which his Jewish audience would have understood *perfectly*.

This "Son of Man" had both divine and human qualities, and in Jewish history, he was promised to not only rule over and above King Nebuchadnezzar (try saying that five times fast), but over the *entire earth*. The "right hand of Power" meant the Son of Man was a figure at the right hand of God. And "coming on the clouds of heaven" was a sign of divine, kingly authority over all the globe. Jesus wasn't pulling this line from the book of Daniel by accident; he was answering their question. In essence, this was the gist: "Not only am I the Christ of the *Jews*, as you say, but my place is at the right hand of the Father, and my kingly authority spreads well beyond you, over the *whole world*." Hmm. Here we see Jesus not just as the ultimate prophet, but the ultimate king too—yet another office of his people's history that he was fulfilling and succeeding in, where past kings had failed. We also see here yet another instance of Jesus' masterful use of Scripture to cleverly communicate things, and this was no exception.

It was more than enough for Caiaphas.

Blasphemy! Blasphemy! he cried, tearing his robes in a show of outrage, an act which was actually forbidden for a priest. He now felt his case against Jesus was sewn up, ready to package and pass along to the full Sanhedrin. "He deserves death," the other elders in attendance chimed in, even as they spat in Jesus' face and slapped him from behind (vv. 65–67).

Friday morning dawned. By now word had spread, and masses of people had arrived to see it for themselves. Judas, perhaps realizing the gravity of his betrayal, brought the thirty pieces of silver back. It was the price of a slave. "I have sinned by betraying innocent blood," he pleaded (Matt. 27:4), desperate to take it all back.

But they refused. They had gotten what they wanted from him, and they had no need for the money or the man. Judas had been used, and he had kissed the hand that would soon be pierced for him.

When he ran away, he flung the coins across the floor, sending them clattering at their feet as he reeled away, unhinged, inconsolable. It would be one of the last things he heard before hanging himself.

But even with things moving forward in their favor, the Sanhedrin, like all politicians, remained sensitive to their poll numbers. For though they were obsessed with wanting Jesus dead, they didn't really want to look like they were the ones behind it. Might look unseemly. Might tarnish their long-standing, long-tasseled, law-abiding image. So, they decided to bring in the Roman governor, Pontius Pilate, as the bad guy. Let him be the one who signs the papers for it. Let him be the one that everybody blames.

After all, Jesus claimed he was a divine king of not just the Jews but the whole world, over and above even Pilate, even Caesar. So, let *him* deal with this guy. Surely, if Jesus claimed as much in front of Pilate, this whole plot would be wrapped up and completed by suppertime.

Remember now, there was also another issue here. If you recall, the Jews were under Roman control at the time. And even though the Romans gave them room to do their own religious stuff most of the time, the Jews had to bring all political matters to them. In other words, the Jews didn't have the authority to put Jesus to death. Only the Romans could do that.

So, they made their case by trying to convince Pilate that Jesus was "misleading our nation and forbidding us to give tribute to Caesar, and saying that he himself is Christ, a king" (Luke 23:2). Did you catch that? "Our" nation? No Jew would ever have wanted to be associated with the Romans in that way. But it sure came in handy now, pretending they cared about how it could adversely affect the empire. Not to mention their inclusion of the word *king*. Surely, they said, this whole thing should be perceived as enough of a threat to the throne of Caesar that Rome would want to stamp out the fire of this rogue Jewish rabbi.

By including both of these words, they were making it easy for Pilate to do something, whether motivated by putting down the uprising of a political rebel, putting out a fire of public disturbance, or squelching anyone who deemed himself a higher noble authority than Caesar. They hoped, in bringing this matter to his attention, Pilate would see they were just doing him a service. *Looking out for your best interests here, sir.*

Except that in examining him, Pilate couldn't come up with anything wrong that Jesus was doing. "I find no guilt in this man," he said (Luke 23:4). *But he's stirring up the people! Don't you see that? He's been doing it all over the place, from here all the way up into Galilee!*

Oh, Galilee, he thought. That was Herod's jurisdiction. Pilate could send him there instead. Let Herod deal with this mess. Why hadn't he thought of this sooner?

So basically, he was sending Jesus to the son of the *other* Herod, the one who'd tried to murder him as a child. Fantastic. This was his youngest son, Herod Antipas, the one who cut off John the Baptist's head and gave it to his stepdaughter on a platter. (Don't tell me I skipped that story too. Sorry. These people were as delightful as they were moral, huh?) But even Herod, like Pilate, couldn't find anything punishable in Jesus. He appeased Pilate by having Jesus beaten, but the Jewish leaders refused to be pacified.

Pilate was now between a rock and a hard place. He knew they'd be furious with him if he let Jesus live. But not only could he see no reason for doing anything else, his wife had awakened from a dream in the night that scared her to death about what would happen if her husband took any action against him: "Have nothing to do with that righteous man," she sent to him in a message, right while he was out there trying to decide what to do (Matt. 27:19).

That's when he thought of a workaround that was sure to fix the problem.

Every year at the Jewish Passover, he customarily released one person from jail. Artificial act of goodwill? Yes, but everybody seemed to like it. How about if he told them *this* year they had a choice between either Jesus (who surely seemed harmless) or Barabbas, one of the most notorious murderers ever caught. Surely, they'd pick Jesus, right? *Nobody* would want Barabbas out on the loose again, would they?

"Who do you choose to be released?"

Barabbas! Barabbas! Give us Barabbas!

"And what do you want me to do with the Christ?"
Crucify him!!!

But why? Pilate begged to know. What had Jesus done to them that was so bad? "I have found in him no guilt deserving death," he said (Luke 23:22), as he publicly washed his hands—a sign that he was taking no part in this.

Yet, again, there's another layer to this story.

Imagine Barabbas, the worst of the worst. A murderer. A dangerous, feared man who'd been rightfully imprisoned for his heinous crimes—the kind of person who truly deserved to die. Imagine him sitting there in his prison cell, near enough to hear the ruckus outside. He knows they're coming to get him, perhaps at any moment, to walk him to his death. While everyone cheers.

He hears his name being chanted: *Barabbas! Barabbas!* It's time. He knows it. *Crucify him! Crucify him!* He steadies himself, taking long breaths and waiting for the sound of the door to swing open.

It does. He looks down. He doesn't want to admit he's terrified.

As the cell door squeaks open, he stands to face his fate.

Barabbas? the jailer says—*you're free to go.*

There he stands. A guilty man. A man with blood on his hands and evil in his heart.

And herein lies the gospel.

Grace came at a cost, and it was all because the innocent One stood in place of the man who should have been crucified.

THE CROSS

The Roman executioners were all too happy to take Jesus into their care. They stripped him naked, beat him mercilessly, and mocked him by setting up a royal scene complete with a scarlet robe and a crown of thorns, making fun of the fact that he had been called a king. They spit on him and kicked him, while the crowd screamed in celebration. As far as the mob was concerned, he was worthy of whatever he got.

Soon a crossbar was strapped across his back, the splinters tearing into his broken flesh. He staggered underneath the weight, having lost so much blood, so they pulled an onlooker from the crowd to help him carry it the rest of the way. As they reached Golgotha—"The Place of a Skull" (John 19:17)—Jesus watched the soldiers finishing their preparations. Tradition said that the name written atop the cross referred to the charge against the sinner. In this case, Pilate wrote, "Jesus of Nazareth, the King of the Jews." But the Jews were furious at this. They yelled for the inscription to be changed. This man wasn't the king of the Jews; he was a blasphemous man who *said* he was king of the Jews! But Pilate responded, "What I have written I have written" (John 19:19–22). Jesus would be killed for being exactly who he was.

Having nailed him to the cross, the soldiers then decided to split all of his clothes into four shares. But one item remained—a seamless tunic that they didn't want to rip up. Instead, they cast lots for it. Essentially, they were drawing straws to see who would get the Messiah's robe.

And this is where the weave of ancient prophecies begins to tighten into place. Remember the book of Psalms? Written hundreds of years before all this? The following verse might mean more to you now, now that you've seen it come to life with such prophetic precision: "They divide my garments among them, and for my clothing they cast lots" (Ps. 22:18). How could David have known what he was writing about, a thousand years before Jesus ever came? He simply wrote down what God had inspired him to say, but it was already part of a redemptive plan. Never in doubt, only in waiting.

The Son of God was killed between two common criminals, fulfilling Isaiah's prophecy that he would be "numbered with the transgressors" (Isa. 53:12). One of the two thieves, even as he hung there dying, believed Jesus' claims of being the Son of God: "Remember me when you come into your kingdom," to which Jesus answered, "Today you will be with me in paradise" (Luke 23:42–43).

But the people's cries of scorn kept filling the darkening skies. They reached an all-time volume as Jesus pressed his feet into the wood, trying to keep himself from suffocating. Being the day before the Jewish Sabbath, the executioners wanted the victims to die quickly because the bodies of convicted men weren't allowed to stay hanging there over the weekend. So if they didn't die fast enough on their own, the attending soldier would break their legs, taking away their ability to raise themselves up.

This meant time was running short for *another* prophecy to be fulfilled. According to Exodus 12:46, the Passover lamb was always to be killed without breaking any of its bones. He was also offered sour wine, in fulfillment of Psalm 69:21: "for my thirst they gave me sour wine to drink"—but he refused it. The wine was intended to dull the pain, but Jesus had come to the cross to feel all the pain for all of us.

Yet somewhere in the crowd, one particular woman was seeing this whole scene differently than everyone else. This was the woman who used to scratch his head when he left the house in the morning, right there on that spot where the crown was now pressing into him. She used to hold his hands in hers, those hands that were now pierced with nails, front to back. She knew the way those hands used to splash in the water and hold a hammer. Now his murderers were the ones holding it. And she could do nothing about it, could do nothing to stop them.

But actually, she'd *never* had a say in the matter, this woman whom God had chosen to bring his Son into the world. She was a "handmaid of the Lord," she said (Luke 1:38 KJV). Whatever his will, it would also be hers. And now here she stood, watching Jesus being brought *out* of the world, again not having a say in the matter.

I want to scream when I think about it. I want to scream and fight to get to him, same as I would if he were a child of mine. But that's not where the thread of God's story was leading—to a last-second rescue, to a deathless redemption. The spotless, righteous Lamb of God must suffer. *Like this.* And die. *Like this.* Our job is not to get in between God and his timeless plan for our salvation. This was the plan agreed upon by both the Father and the Son. Yes, the Father sent his Son, but at the same time, the Son also willingly volunteered. And the Holy Spirit? He empowered it all. The Trinity was in perfect agreement over this. And I don't know about you, but I don't think trying to get in the way of the Trinity's plan for something is ever going to work out well.

Our job is only to sit back and wonder, and worship, and *believe* that the One who tied this whole story together and into our time line has done it because of that same passionate pursuit he's been showing us in Scripture since the garden of Eden.

God comes. God bends low. God pursues his fallen people.

"Father, forgive them, for they know not what they do," Jesus said (Luke 23:34), his blood staining the ground, another of the seven total statements the Bible says he made from the cross that day. "I thirst," he said (John 19:28), struggling for air as his body weakened. When he caught sight of Mary standing in anguish beside his friend John, he appealed to her, "Woman, behold your son!" and to his beloved disciple, "Behold, your mother!" (John 19:26–27).

By around 3:00, with the entire land now shrouded in a thick, heavy darkness, Jesus spoke those heartbreaking words, "My God, my God, why have you forsaken me?" (Matt. 27:46)—the desperate cry of a Son wanting to be with his Father. Instead of the closeness of God, he was feeling the wrath of God. He was experiencing our shame. And he was experiencing it as a man—feeling all the agony for all the sin that he had willingly agreed to take upon his shoulders. The separation from God was unbearable. It's the only time in Scripture that Jesus didn't call God his Father. The weight of every sin—all of yours and all of mine—balanced there, sagging there, tormenting him there between two narrow beams of wood.

Finally, it was done. Someone in the audience lifted to him a sponge of wine, perched on top of a hyssop branch—the same branch used for smearing the blood of the Passover lamb over their doors in Egypt, generations before. Now the Lamb and his blood were delivering not just the Hebrews, but the entire world, from the slavery of sin.

"Father, into your hands I commit my spirit!" (Luke 23:46), he screamed, before finally declaring, "It is finished" (John 19:30). He took his last breath, the Savior of the world. The promised Christ. The Lord of all things.

Historians have noted that an extraordinary eclipse of the sun occurred on this day. They say the stars in heaven could be seen in the middle of the afternoon—the same stars that hung above Abraham, the stars that set the backdrop for a covenant that was now being fulfilled hundreds of years later. The sky was dark and the ground was trembling. And in that moment, something else happened—something that would allow us to enter the holiest place, the presence of God himself.

Do you remember the tabernacle? The Holy of Holies, where a veil kept everyone but the high priest from the presence of God? It was to separate the sinful people from God's holy presence, and it had been that way for hundreds and hundreds of years.

I told you that you'd understand this later, and I hope you'll see why as you read this next part.

As Jesus cried out his dying words, the Bible says the sound of a seamless curtain being torn in half echoed throughout the temple.

From top to bottom.

From heaven to earth.

Now that sin had been paid for, nothing else could separate us, whether Jew or Gentile, from entering in and receiving mercy. Usually only a priest could mediate between the two, but now Jesus—our ultimate priest—became the world's mediator to the Father. He removed the barrier of sin that was holding us back, so that through him we could access the Father's throne in full confidence.

Jesus obeyed God perfectly because we couldn't. And through his sacrifice, our slate isn't just wiped clean; it's filled with Jesus' obedient record. When God looks at you, *that's* what he sees. A divine transaction happened on that cross: your sin for his righteousness. He took your record and gave you his in return.

And get this—Jesus didn't just play the divine and final roles of obedient child, prophet, king, and priest (all the roles that God's people had failed to fulfill properly before him). He also played the role of the sacrifice itself. He was the unblemished, spotless, righteous One on the altar—all for us. Remember the covenant God made many chapters before now—the one that said, "if you get this wrong, *I'll* pay for it, in a manner similar to these sacrificial animals?" Jesus was keeping that end of the bargain. Instead of making us pay for our failure to keep our end of the deal, he paid for it. Yes, the Lamb of God had paved the way, by his blood, for anyone in all the world to come and be forgiven.

THE RESURRECTION

It had been only a week since Jesus rode into Jerusalem on a donkey, and now he'd been crucified and buried just outside of town. It's interesting to note that the two men who removed his body from the cross were two members of the Sanhedrin—Nicodemus, a man who first came to Jesus in John 3, trying to come to grips with what belief might mean, as well as Joseph of Arimathea, another man who hadn't voted in favor of Jesus' crucifixion and who happened to own a newly cut tomb. Again, as the Bible had said, the Messiah would make his grave "with a rich man in his death" (Isa. 53:9). The prophecies just keep on falling into place.

The task of removing a body was not easy. They may have had to hammer the nails back through his wrists the opposite way. They surely were covered in the blood that had saved them. Jesus was unrecognizable by now. His eyes were closed. His mouth was motionless. His bruises and swelling had stolen any physical semblance of the man they'd known and come to believe in. As they lowered him from the cross, they were bearing the weight of a man who had just borne the weight of the world. With Sabbath approaching, there wasn't time to anoint his body with the proper spices, but simply wrap him and make plans to return and finish what needed to be done for a proper burial.

In keeping with tradition dictated upon the death of a loved one, several women who had followed Jesus arose bright and early on the day after Sabbath. They weren't sure how they would get to him. They knew a massive stone had been placed in front of his tomb, and guards were standing by to make sure his followers didn't come steal the body, pretending he'd been resurrected.

But when they got there, they stood amazed.

The stone had been rolled away.

Stricken by the thought that either thieves or animals had done something destructive to his body, they peered warily into the tomb, terrified at what they'd find. Inside were two angels, who told them not to be afraid: "For I know that you seek Jesus who was crucified. He is not here, for he has risen" (Matt. 28:5–6).

The women ran to tell of the miracle.

He was risen.

Three small words that made the story true. If it had just been a crucifixion, the prophecies would not have been fulfilled. But death could not hold down the Son of God. We don't know the exact moment of his first earthly breath when he was born, and we don't know the exact time of his first breath after resurrection. But what we do know, and what we cling to as his followers, is that both of them happened.

Humankind has two major problems: (1) our debt of sin that needs paying for, and (2) that big, huge curse called death. If we remember all the way back to the garden, death wasn't supposed to be a thing. Humans weren't ever supposed to die. We were created to live forever. But sin brought in the age of death. And until someone defeated it, we had no hope of eternal life in a resurrected, immortal state. We'd have no way of going back to the way things were supposed to be all along unless somebody dealt with death and reversed it.

The cross is where the penalty for sin was paid for. That's where our number-one problem got fixed.

But God never does things halfway. The resurrection is where God bested death. The gospel is not only where sin was paid for, once and for all, but where death was defeated, opening a way for us, too, to one day be resurrected and live forever on a new, non-cursed, flourishing earth.

Not to mention, if Jesus didn't rise from the dead, he wouldn't be alive right now in order to hear your prayers and intercede for you, and reign over the world, and work in your life, and do all the other things he promises he's doing for you *right this very minute*. Our King isn't a dead teacher whose ways we follow, as many religious figures of history are. No, he is alive, active, and working in our lives now because he got out of the grave two thousand years ago.

Glory be to God. We are not only freed from sin, and yet still destined to be buried one day and lost to history. We are invited by our risen King to rise too—into an eternity of life and peace.

DON'T DOUBT, JUST BELIEVE

I've mentioned earlier that I have some favorite Bible stories (plural). I guess I just have issues with the kind of commitment that would force me to narrow down my selection to only one. After all, I might change my mind someday before they carve my tombstone, and it would be such a mess to switch it out.

So since I'm leaving myself some leeway here, I'd like to submit for "favorite" consideration today a story from John 20 that features one of Jesus' twelve disciples in a supporting role.

I say "supporting" on purpose because, to me, I think this particular disciple gets a bad rap. He's known almost universally today as "doubting Thomas," but he was actually a truly loyal follower of Christ. As a means of defending that position, I enter into evidence a lesser known scene from John 11, when some of Jesus' other disciples were showing their cowardly, clueless side, trying to talk him out of a trip that they thought would put all of them unnecessarily in harm's way. Thomas said, *no, come on, let's go!*—"that we may die with him" (v. 16).

Daring, not doubting.

But by John 20, Jesus was dead. Even though his disciples and many others had seen the resurrected Christ, Thomas refused to believe them. I just don't think he could accept it without at least a twinge of honest skepticism. "Unless I see in his hands the mark of the nails, and place my finger into the mark of the nails, and place my hand into his side," he said, "I will never believe" (v. 25).

See, I don't think that's such a ridiculous thing to say. Because while I realize he went off on a bit of a tirade there—a crisis of faith—the root of his crisis doesn't sound like *unbelief* to me. It just sounds like a deep, heart desire to believe more fully. And I get that. I can relate to Thomas. Because whenever I question God (and I do), I'm not trying to prove he doesn't exist. I ask questions of him and ask questions about him because I genuinely want to rest in unshakable faith.

And I believe the same was true of Thomas. I mean, follow his actions, not merely his words. He continued to hang with his disciple buddies, even though he hadn't yet seen Jesus alive with his own eyes. It wasn't as though he'd abandoned his confidence in what Jesus had said and meant to them. And when the resurrected Lord unexpectedly showed up eight days after the other disciples had seen Jesus, I'm sure Thomas was in awe.

And I love this next part. It would be easy to miss as you're just reading along with the text, but I spend a lot of time with the doubters of the Bible, so maybe I notice some of the details that matter to me as a person who relates.

Are you ready for this?

The first thing Jesus did as he entered the house was to greet everybody. Then, immediately after that, he spoke five words that are a pretty unlikely "favorite Bible verse" choice, and yet I submit them to you anyway. "Then he said to Thomas . . ." The gaze of heaven turned to the one who doubted. Not to rebuke him, but to encourage him to believe.

> "Put your finger here, and see my hands; and put out your hand, and place it in my side. Do not disbelieve, but believe." (John 20:27)

First of all, how did Jesus know this was exactly what Thomas had said he needed to see? Jesus wasn't there when Thomas had made his requests. He was being very deliberate as he recited them back to him for this reason. But the next thing we hear is not the sound of Thomas's feet, moving in closer to investigate, demanding to see the proof he'd asked for. There's no evidence that he ever touched Jesus, despite the fact that he'd claimed it was the only way he would ever believe. (It's another one of those, "But I thought the Bible said that!!!" It doesn't. Go make sure your nativity goats are in one piece.) I suppose being in the presence of the living God erased all the conditions Thomas had put in place. Instead, we hear only the sound of his voice, speaking words that had never been uttered before: "My Lord and my God!" (v. 28). No one had ever called Jesus both Lord *and* God.

The doubter became the declarer.

Some of us, like Thomas, are wired to want all the proof we can get, evidence of Jesus' life and death that we can hold up in front of others and say, "See? This is something you can believe in." Yet what we learn from Thomas's story is that, while observable facts are fine as far as they go, not even Christ's physical hands and feet are enough for those people who have no real intention of being turned from their doubts. But to those who truly want to believe— who want to believe more fully—God will always give enough. Not as much as we may want, perhaps, but always more than we need.

As he said by way of gentle reminder to Thomas, "Blessed are those who have not seen and yet have believed" (v. 29). These words are for us as well—the ones who didn't see, and yet choose to believe.

Chapter 13

JUST TRY STOPPING US NOW
The Church

 The message of Christ was soon to begin traveling far and wide, but it wouldn't be without obstacles. Before we get into that, let's make sure we're on the same page as far as definitions of terms.

We're moving past the *Gospels* at this point—the specific, capital-G "Gospels"—the four books of the Bible that tell the story of Jesus' life on this physical planet. But that part of his story is actually the fulfillment of a larger *gospel* (again, that's the Greek word for "good news"), a story that stretches all the way back to the beginning of time and weaves its way through Christ's earthly life and beyond. The gospel was already the gospel before he ever came here as a man, before the calendar BC became the calendar AD. But in coming and living the gospel out, Jesus filled the gospel with himself.

> In him all the fullness of God was pleased to dwell, and through him to reconcile to himself all things, whether on earth or in heaven, making peace by the blood of his cross.
>
> And you, who once were alienated and hostile in mind, doing evil deeds, he has now reconciled in his body of flesh by his death, in order to present you holy and blameless and above reproach before him,

233

> if indeed you continue in the faith, stable
> and steadfast, not shifting from the hope of
> the gospel that you heard, which has been
> proclaimed in all creation under heaven.
> (Col. 1:19–23)

All right, hold up for a sec. I want you to know, straight out, I forgive you if you couldn't close this book right now and tell me *one thing* those verses just said.

I know, I do it myself. It's easy to autopilot these things.

But, humor me. Go back and give it another shot, will you?—because all the essential parts of the gospel are in there, inside that little block of verses. Jesus, the Son of God, came here to rescue us, people who were "alienated and hostile" toward him, enslaved to our sins. And he created a way, the only way, that we by our faith in him can be purified and at peace with God.

That's talking about you and me—who, we know, from way too much firsthand experience, are the most stubborn, selfish, stinking people we know. Yet even we—*even I*—have been declared through Christ "holy and blameless and above reproach before him."

But not only do we get to believe it, we get to live it. We get to "continue" in it, "stable and steadfast," out in those everyday, sometimes faraway places where believing faith becomes living hope—hope that "will not disappoint us," the Bible says, "because God's love has been poured out in our hearts" (Rom. 5:5 csb).

With that said, Jesus left us with hard truth about our lives as his followers:

> "They will deliver you up to tribulation and
> put you to death, and you will be hated by
> all nations for my name's sake. And then
> many will fall away and betray one another
> and hate one another. And many false

prophets will arise and lead many astray. And because lawlessness will be increased, the love of many will grow cold." (Matt. 24:9–12)

"But," Jesus promised, "the one who endures to the end will be saved" (v. 13). The gospel, he told them, would be strong and empowering enough to take them through hell on earth and still make them victorious over it, not only in the end but at every step of the way. "And this gospel of the kingdom will be proclaimed throughout the whole world as a testimony to all nations" (v. 14) so that everyone can know the same freedom and confidence and resilience of faith in Christ for themselves.

That's what we can take from the remaining books of the New Testament. Let's take a closer look at them, although I think you at least have a good idea of what they talk about.

Following Jesus' resurrection, as the Gospels surged to a close, the risen Christ gave his followers an extremely important charge:

> "All authority in heaven and on earth has been given to me. Go therefore and make disciples of all nations, baptizing them in the name of the Father and of the Son and of the Holy Spirit, teaching them to observe all that I have commanded you. And behold, I am with you always, to the end of the age." (Matt. 28:18–20)

This biblical mandate is what's known today as the Great Commission. Jesus was clear that their task was to go tell everyone about him—every tribe, every nation, everyone, everywhere. As recipients of the gospel, their job was to spread it and share it wherever they went.

Big job, huh? So, no way was he dropping that huge responsibility on his few little followers' shoulders and then just sending them off with a sack lunch and a pat on the head. Something big was coming, he said. They would not be going out alone, *trust me.* "I am sending the promise of my Father upon you" (Luke 24:49)—a promise he'd mentioned to them repeatedly during that long passage from John on the Thursday night of Passover, if they'd been paying attention. Of course, we can't assume they actually picked up on what he meant.

We're about to jump into some uncharted territory here, so I'm going to warn you: this is a topic that scholars trip over as they try to define it perfectly. It can't be done. It's part of the beautiful mystery of God.

"When the Helper comes," he had said, "the Spirit of truth, who proceeds from the Father, he will bear witness about me. And you also will bear witness, because you have been with me from the beginning" (John 15:26–27). Or as he'd said even more recently, *after* his resurrection, immediately *before* he ascended bodily into heaven:

> "You will receive power when the Holy Spirit has come upon you, and you will be my witnesses in Jerusalem and in all Judea and Samaria, and to the end of the earth." (Acts 1:8)

Jerusalem, Judea, and from there to the rest of the world. Jesus was spreading out the map for the gospel's expansion plans. Widening the circle.

But first—extremely important, he told them—"stay in the city until you are clothed with power from on high" (Luke 24:49b). Don't go anywhere, kids. Not yet.

They stuck it out, "devoting themselves to prayer, together with the women and Mary the mother of Jesus, and his brothers" (Acts 1:14).

Then it happened. And it was NOT A SUBTLE MOMENT.

Many Jews had once again gathered in Jerusalem from all over, this time for the celebration of Pentecost, another festival with deep Old Testament roots. In earlier times it was known as the "Feast of Harvest" (Exod. 23:16) or the "day of the firstfruits" (Num. 28:26). It was a time of thanksgiving to God for the first crops of the season, celebrated fifty days after Passover. (That's how it came to be known as *Pentecost,* a Greek term coined to mean "fifty days.")

Or you could think of it this way: it was a "week of weeks" after Passover—forty-nine days plus one, for a total of seven weeks. *Seven,* I bet you remember, was considered the number of perfection, of completion. So there's lots of cool imagery tied up in Pentecost. In retrospect, you can see why God chose it as the "perfect" moment to do something spiritually significant.

Like bringing in the first "harvest" of new souls into the kingdom. (Is that not beautiful?)

Yes, and here's how he did it.

> When the day of Pentecost arrived, they were all together in one place. And suddenly there came from heaven a sound like a mighty rushing wind, and it filled the entire house where they were sitting. (Acts 2:1–2)

Pure, explosive power. The Holy Spirit demonstrably fell upon them, filling them with the Spirit of God himself. And yes, as believers in Christ, that same Holy Spirit takes up residence in us when we declare our need for him, repenting of our sin and believing that Jesus is who he says he is.

But the scene was so crazy the first time it happened that people thought they were drunk. And it wasn't just locals who were there; many had traveled to Jerusalem at that time, who then took this living gospel to their towns and people.

Also, Peter . . .

Remember the last time we saw Peter? Of course you do. He was skulking around in the shadows, somewhere outside the house where Jesus was being skewered with questions. Peter was denying he could ever have been seen with the man. But now he was unstoppable, telling them, *Christ is real. This is what happened. And I saw it with my own eyes.*

So, in case you're wondering, doubt doesn't keep you from becoming a bold witness for God. Neither does a moment of weakness when you say things you wish you hadn't said and you grieve over them. Peter was filled with the Holy Spirit that day—meaning, although he was as naturally weak and fearful as any of the rest of us, he was borrowing from a boldness given to him by God himself.

Borrowing boldness.

What a beautiful gift his Spirit offers to us.

It made him courageous enough to say to the gathered masses, "Repent and be baptized every one of you in the name of Jesus Christ for the forgiveness of your sins, and you *[too]* will receive the gift of the Holy Spirit" (Acts 2:38).

He then added a line I do not want you to miss. He said he wasn't merely speaking that day to the people who were standing there in front of him, whose feet were planted right that moment in Jerusalem. He wasn't weaving only *them* into the story; he was weaving *us* into the story, into this gospel story.

"For the promise is for you and for your
children and for all who are far off, everyone whom the Lord our God calls to himself." (v. 39)

Everyone. Everywhere. You. Me. Everybody.
The Holy Spirit brings *all* who believe into the story.

ACTION

I'm sure you noticed we've now been dipping into the
book of Acts, the fifth book in the New Testament. And
here's the thing. Unlike the Old Testament, which has a lot
of books of history, Acts is the only dedicated history book
in the remainder of the New Testament. It tells the "Acts"
of the first Christians, of the early church. In fact, the title
page in your Bible may actually call it "The Acts of the
Apostles." The *apostles* were people who personally knew
the man Jesus and helped the first generation of Christ-
followers establish their faith.

Oh, and here's another thing. Acts was written by our
good friend Dr. Luke, did you know that? So you can think
of it as the sequel to his Gospel. Which means you can
expect it to be rich in texture and detail. *And it is.* The book
of Acts is a really good read. You'll love it.

I don't need to tell you, though, the ending of Acts
leaves us with twenty-two additional books that fill out the
New Testament.

And now we're all set to go over every single one of
them in meticulous detail, down to the kind of parchment
paper Luke was using to transfer the words he'd been
given. Don't worry, I'm not going to do that. But we *are*
going to hop on a couple of story stones along the way.

Here's the deal, though. You need to pinky-promise
me that you will read them all. *Gah!* Based on what you've

already learned and are about to learn, they'll mean so much to you.

Okay, now you may remember our having this same sort of discussion when we were going through the Old Testament and when we reached the end of its historical books as well. The part from Romans to Revelation is not an extension of the New Testament narrative. Rather, like the books of Old Testament prophecy, we can sort of shuffle the remaining books into the same history that the book of Acts talks about.

I know this horse has been dead since Genesis, but I'm going to say it again: the Bible is not in order. So when you open to the part we're about to talk about, you'll see that there are many books (which are actually just letters written by individuals to either churches or other individuals). Don't assume they're happening chronologically. They're actually mostly ordered from shortest to longest, so we're just going to tell the story and insert them where they happened, okay?

Don't pull a Thomas. I'm not lying to you. Here, touch my appendix to prove it. Can I let you in on a little writer's secret? We have rare moments in our work where we actually laugh at our own selves and pat ourselves on the back when we think we wrote something clever. For the record, connecting the appendix (body part) with the appendix (part of a book) is pretty darn good.

High five to me.

Moving on . . .

So, here's what's left, by way of category:

- Paul's Letters to Churches (nine books: Romans through 2 Thessalonians)
- Paul's Letters to Individuals (four books: 1 Timothy through Philemon)

- General Letters (Hebrews, James, Peter and John's letters, Jude)
- Prophecy (only one book: Revelation, also written by John)

I know we haven't met Paul yet. We will, because no book about the Bible should leave him out. Oh, my goodness, JUST WAIT. As you can see from the sheer volume of his contribution to the biblical literature (thirteen books in total), there's no way to understand the New Testament without grasping his major role in it. Not just because of who he was, as a person, but because of how God specifically chose and employed him to spread the news about a gospel "mystery"—exactly what the Bible calls it—that would forever change not only our lives but the whole world. (*Tip: if anyone quotes you a line from the New Testament and asks who said it, Paul is a super solid guess.)

Here's why his influence is so important. Among the parts of the gospel that make it so magnificent is one which, up until Paul's day, would've been considered completely irrational. It's this: the good news of God's love and favor extends to ALL who believe. Not only the Jews but also the Gentiles.

And, again, we citizens of the twenty-first century simply don't have a real frame of reference for understanding how radical—R-A-D-I-C-A-L—this idea sounded at the time.

The Jews were the ones who maintained the traditions of the law. The Jews were the ones known throughout the annals of history as God's especially chosen people. They'd been awaiting their Messiah, their Savior, for many centuries, waiting for him to stride heroically onto the stage, restore them to a place of cultural and military dominance, and trod their enemies fully and forever under their feet.

Problem was, their enemies were not who they thought they were. The enemy of the Jews was actually the same as that of the Gentiles. The chief enemy that every one of us faces is the enemy of our own indwelling sin. Doesn't matter who we are or where we come from. And when Jesus came and died on the cross, his sacrifice of blood defeated *that* enemy. For all of us.

This is ground-shifting theology.

And here's a reminder from the last chapter. The way we gain access into this heart-changing, mind-changing, entire-destiny-changing experience is not by keeping the law of Moses, or by filling up the check boxes on our religious score sheet and working to become good people. Remember? Jesus, having fulfilled the law perfectly, invites us to let *his* perfect righteousness be counted as *our* perfect righteousness. And so by faith in him, as opposed to working for him, we are freed to live in real-time victory. Despite how we feel, despite how we fail, we can legitimately consider ourselves "dead to sin and alive to God in Christ Jesus" (Rom. 6:11).

And *anyone* is welcome to it. As far as the gospel is concerned, "there is neither Jew nor Greek, there is neither slave nor free, there is no male and female, for you are all one in Christ Jesus." God's chosen people, as it turns out, are all those who believe in him. "If you are Christ's, then you are Abraham's offspring, heirs according to promise" (Gal. 3:28–29).

I AM SO PRAYING THAT IF YOU'D READ THIS VERSE PRIOR TO READING THIS BOOK, IT NOW MEANS MORE TO YOU BECAUSE YOU HAVE CONTEXT.

The gospel is open to all, my friend. To all who receive his grace by faith.

The curtain has been torn.

But this free-to-all, grace-based aspect of the gospel is also what leaves it open to controversy. From all sides. As life-giving as the gospel becomes for those whose hearts are transformed by it, the gospel is equally as irritating and repulsive to those who refuse it, to those who refuse him.

And that's the powder-keg reality into which the apostles took their obedience to the Great Commission. People weren't always welcoming of their message. The young, developing church could cause quite a stir, to the point of people accusing them of having "turned the world upside down" (Acts 17:6). They gathered steam and new converts among some people, but met with stiff headwinds of persecution from others. In fact, by as early as Acts 7, the Bible identifies the first of its many martyrs: an irrepressible, Spirit-empowered believer named Stephen.

But don't think God wasn't at work, even in tragedy. Because off to the side, almost out of camera range, while these enemies of the gospel were seeking to silence this preacher's voice with their hard-thrown rocks, an obscure young Pharisee was holding the murderers' coats for them, someone who fully approved of this execution.

It's our first meet-up with Paul.

Oh my gosh, Paul.

I LOVE YOU, PAUL!!!!! (*Tries to get autograph by shoving headshot in his face as he exits the venue.)

No, I don't love what he was doing at this minute, of course, but I love that God still had an enormous plan for him, despite where he came from.

Now during his first appearances in Scripture, Luke called Paul by his Hebrew name, Saul. As time went on, however, and his name became almost synonymous with the spread of the gospel among the Gentiles, Luke began referring to him by the Greek iteration of his name: Paul.

First, though, let me introduce you to the "Saul" part.

Saul of Tarsus came from a regional capital located northwest of Palestine, along the upper coast of the

Mediterranean. He was a Roman citizen. But he was a devout Jew who'd been trained by one of the most highly respected rabbis around. As a result, Saul, like many others of his day, saw Christianity as a threat to both the purity of Jewish faith and to the role that the law of Moses was meant to play in the corporate life of their communities. And yet unlike some, this wasn't just his kinda-sorta, kicking-the-ball-around opinion. It wasn't something that came up in conversation only when he was chatting with his buddies about current events over lunch. No, Saul ate, drank, and slept his opposition to Christianity. He was an active persecutor of the church. He set out on personal vigilante missions to smoke them out, round them up, and haul them off to jail. To death. Whatever it took.

He was a staunch, vocal enemy of everything Jesus.

That's why he was present when Stephen, the first martyr, was murdered for his faith.

Why then would God, when he set out to recruit his first major missionary, his leading spokesman for the gospel, the one whose influence would be more widely felt around the world than any other single person—why would his eye turn to Saul as the perfect man for the job?

I'll tell you why. Because in his unconventional, unexpected, nobody-other-than-God way, he wanted to pick the least likely candidate. Remember Jacob the trickster? Rahab the prostitute? Remember *Jesus*? Unlikely, unlikely, unlikely. This is such a theme in the Bible. God wanted someone whose very presence as a hater, a persecutor, and a devout unbeliever would be visible proof of what God's grace can actually do. His choice of Paul is one of the main stories of the Bible that gives me hope for my life and my usefulness to God.

He wanted Saul of Tarsus?

Maybe he could even want me.

And in just a minute here, God was about to speak to this man that no one else would've chosen for the job. Sometimes it takes a hammer falling on your head during home renovation to get the point. And this was even more drastic.

God blinded Saul.

There, within a darkness of his own making, the risen Christ himself spoke words that would shape the rest of Scripture, and of time: "Saul, Saul, why are you persecuting me?" (Acts 9:4).

Saul responded, "Who are you, Lord?"—to which our Savior replied, "I am Jesus, whom you are persecuting" (v. 5). He told Saul that he was his chosen instrument, and that he would carry the message of the gospel to the world. Saul received the Holy Spirit and immediately began preaching the good news in everything he did, in any way he could. And since he'd encountered the risen Christ and had been tasked with raising up churches based on faith and belief in Jesus, he could lay claim to being an apostle.

Yet Paul thought of himself, in relation to the twelve apostles, as being one who was "untimely born"—"the least of the apostles, unworthy to be called an apostle, because I persecuted the church of God." And yet "by the grace of God," he said, "I am what I am" (1 Cor. 15:8–10). That's what I love so much about him.

And he never forgot it. He knew—better than most of us know it, I fear—that he had zero redeeming qualities with which to vouch for the loving attention God paid to him. Yet despite what surely must have been enormous pangs of guilt that haunted him from his past, he exhibited the grace-filled attitude of "forgetting what lies behind and straining forward to what lies ahead, I press on toward the goal for the prize of the upward call of God in Christ Jesus" (Phil. 3:13–14).

But when did God change his name?

Well, he didn't. That's a common misconception. Paul/Saul was assigned to speak mostly to Gentiles, and Paul was the version of his name that would be most familiar to them.

Suffice it to say, the book of Acts—from chapter 9 forward—is primarily taken up with Paul's three missionary journeys, concluding with his journey to Italy by boat as an imperial prisoner. The vessel that was carrying him and a couple of hundred others shipwrecked along the way, making the adventure even more fun. (*Eeeekkkk, sorry to be a pain here, but could I be on a different excursion from Paul?) It ended with him under house arrest in Rome but, as usual, he was still "proclaiming the kingdom of God and teaching about the Lord Jesus Christ with all boldness and without hindrance" (Acts. 28:31).

There's so much more I could say about the book of Acts. The struggles and miracles experienced in the early church are insanely fascinating. People look back and think this age of the church was perfect, that these were model days of unity and harmonious fellowship we should all aspire toward. In some ways, yes; in other ways, I don't know. True, we've complicated the simplicity and passion of mission that the first believers lived with. We could afford to rediscover and recover the basics of the early church in this moment. At the same time though, God still clearly wanted to do some more structural forming of his church, or else the rest of the Bible wouldn't exist as Scripture, telling developing churches how to handle things, right? In none of the subsequent letters of the New Testament do we see God saying, "Y'all need to go back to that season of the church's life and history and just do things that way again." And yet, either way, the main thing is this: they needed Jesus; we need Jesus. Our need for him never stops, nor does our mandate for living and championing his gospel at all costs, for his glory.

But there's a lot to learn from reading the book of Acts, a lot to be inspired by. I hope you'll keep it by your bedside and spend some time in it real soon. Here are just a couple of the major threads that run through it, which intersect with Paul's travels to the various churches he started:

1. *The dispersion of believers.* Whereas the Gospels, and even most of the Old Testament, centered geographically around the same basic region of the world, Acts witnesses the explosion of the gospel outward, mostly westward, all the way over into Greece, even to Rome. The Great Commission truly comes to life, and it comes to life *fast* in the pages of Acts.

2. *The division of labor.* This Jew-and-Gentile thing we've been talking about was a huge theological mountain for the people of that era to climb over. You might find it interesting that not even Peter was quick to get on board. His heart really fought with his head. Paul, in fact, writing in Galatians 2, told of a scene where he openly confronted Peter for being all buddy-buddy with the Gentiles when nobody else was around, then clamming up and acting more exclusive toward them when folks from the Jerusalem church showed up.

Acts 10 recounts the story of God calling Peter to go meet with a Roman centurion (a military officer in command of a hundred men), which Peter felt reluctant to do at first. But when he got to the man's house, where the Italian soldier asked him about Jesus, Peter saw with his own eyes that God was as willing to respond to a Gentile's belief as he'd responded to that of the Jews. "Who was I to think that I could stand in God's way?" he concluded (Acts 11:17 NIV). Peter was changing. He was growing.

Yet it remained a sticking point among many. Luke reported on how a number of teachers who'd come to

Christian belief out of a Jewish background were going around to predominantly Gentile churches, saying, "Unless you are circumcised according to the custom of Moses, you cannot be saved" (Acts 15:1).

Again, this is not a strong marketing campaign. And it's also not true, so there's that.

Paul, as you can imagine, was not super pumped about this. It led to a big summit meeting in Jerusalem, presided over by James, the half-brother of Jesus and author of the New Testament book of, you guessed it, James. The group arrived at the prayerful conclusion that this tacking on of old legal conditions as a determiner of authentic Christian faith was an overreach. It was anti-gospel.

PAUL'S FIRST MISSIONARY JOURNEY

But the controversy itself didn't go away. And though Paul's heart remained tender toward and hungry for the Jews to find their true home in Christ, he began focusing his efforts on taking the gospel to the Gentiles, even as Peter and others primarily evangelized among the Jewish population. They divided and conquered, as it were.

That's the broad brush of the book of Acts. And it sets up all the New Testament books that follow.

PAUL'S LETTERS TO THE CHURCHES

We start the homestretch portion of our time together by pulling out another map, seen on the previous page, which shows the circuit Paul took on his first missionary journey. As background, make a note that this series of travels corresponds with events captured in Acts 13–14.

The church in Antioch (you can see the city of Antioch there) was the one that sent him out, along with two other ministry partners: Barnabas, as well as a young man named John Mark. Guess what? John Mark is the "Mark" who wrote the Gospel of Mark. So now you know.

They went around talking about Jesus, when they weren't getting beat up and dodging death threats. (You know, the usual.) But they were plowing hard ground. They were laying down some of the first pieces of track for the gospel to ride across on its way to the nations. Once they'd traveled as far as they felt the Holy Spirit wanted them to go, they doubled back and revisited each city and church on their way home, then got ready to head out and do it all over again.

For his second go-round, Paul chose a man named Silas to come along, after Paul and Barnabas had a bit of a falling out. Barnabas wanted to take John Mark again, who'd bailed on them about halfway through their first mission.

Barnabas was such an encourager. He wanted to give John Mark a second chance. You'd think Paul would appreciate that, since Barnabas had been one of Paul's earliest champions too, back when most church leaders were slow to trust his motives (given his previous years of rabid Christian-hating). Paul, though—let's just say he was a little more Type-A. He was more mission driven. He didn't want to be constantly worrying about somebody quitting on him again.

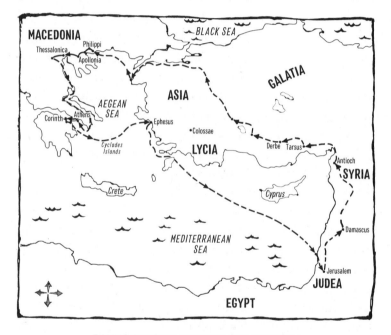

PAUL'S SECOND MISSIONARY JOURNEY

So, the four of them split up, with Paul and Silas going north, overland, headed for even farther destinations than before. (This second missionary journey is chronicled in the last few verses of Acts 15 through most of Acts 18.) Notably, they picked up another church-planting partner along the way, young Timothy, who would become one of Paul's most loyal companions, all the way to his death.

And now we catch up with the first letter Paul wrote.

The reasons for why he wrote these letters to churches varied from place to place. But think about it. He was going into these cities, evangelizing new believers, helping churches get started. But they had questions. Lots of questions. And they had problems. Lots of problems. So even if he were able to stay in one location for weeks or months, he couldn't help counsel them on every potential situation or doctrinal flare-up that might arise. Nor could he foresee every wind of false teaching that might blow into town later, upsetting the unity of the church and impeding the work of the gospel in those areas. But when he'd hear word about these things, out on the road somewhere, he'd fire off a letter and send it back through messengers as a way of keeping communication going.

Folks are pretty sure the first biblical letters Paul wrote are what we now call *1 Thessalonians* and *2 Thessalonians*, sent to new believers in the Greek city of Thessalonica. Both letters mainly deal with the second coming of Jesus, based on some questions the people there were apparently asking. He wanted to keep them from being "shaken in mind or alarmed" (2 Thess. 2:2) about things they'd been hearing from misleading teachers concerning the "day of the Lord" and whether they could count on Christ to take them safely to heaven with him.

Want to learn some stuff about life after death? About Jesus' second coming? (Yes, he's coming back!) Paul's two letters to the Thessalonians are good places to go for that.

Let's stick his letter to the *Galatians* in this spot, too, even though there's dispute over when he visited and wrote to them. Galatia was a whole province, not a single city. I fully realize you bought this book because you were under the impression that I was going to solve this mystery, but alas, I have failed you. The churches Paul established in that region were being badgered by Jewish evangelists, teaching what Paul called a "different gospel" (Gal. 1:6), burdening people with add-on things like circumcision, dietary rules, observance of the religious calendar, and such. Paul didn't mince words about it. He was a *fighter* for the gospel, and he was a fighter for these people whom he'd led to Christ by faith alone. Galatians is sort of a spiritual declaration of independence. "For freedom Christ has set us free," he said, "stand firm therefore, and do not submit again to a yoke of slavery" (Gal. 5:1).

His big point was this: *Jesus freed you from performing your way into the Father's favor. Don't go back to performing again with all these extra add-ons to the gospel! You already have a perfect record. You are free from all that hoop-jumping!*

Paul's original itinerary for his second journey didn't include a western swing into Greece. For some reason, though, he felt the Spirit forbidding him from taking his planned route. Then in a dream one night, he received what he thought to be new instructions. He envisioned a man begging him to "come over to Macedonia and help us" (Acts 16:9). P.S.—that's another one of my recurring dreams.

This is how Paul found himself in cities like Philippi, Thessalonica, and Corinth, as well as Ephesus on the way back, each stop determined by God himself, and each of them carrying all kinds of biblical significance.

Paul's third journey, after only a brief stop in Antioch, was basically a repeat visit to all the places he'd previously been. (It stretches from Acts 18 into Acts 21.)

But it set off his letter-writing campaign in earnest.

First Corinthians was a letter he wrote during that trip, addressing a whole bunch of problems their turbulent congregation was going through. If you ever get discouraged or disillusioned with God's people, with all our imperfections and peculiarities, read 1 Corinthians. Corinth was noooottttt in great shape.

Hoping his letter had done some good, Paul sent a messenger to Corinth to see how things were going. The report came back saying, in essence, "Most everyone in the church gets what you're saying, Paul, but some of them are not sure you're really an apostle. They say they don't know if they should believe you because you're not one of the Twelve that Jesus chose."

Paul, as you may have noticed, was not exactly the "giving up" kind. So, he wrote a follow-up letter (YEAH, HE DID) to explain why his authority as an apostle could be trusted. This letter, of course, following a creative brainstorming session, comes to us with the title of *2 Corinthians*.

Up until this point, up until this question of his legitimacy had come about, Paul had really meant to return to Corinth again. Part of his reason for wanting to go was to gather up their contribution to an offering that he'd been collecting, which he intended to take back to the church in Jerusalem. He saw it as a sign of Gentile solidarity and support for the believing Jews. But fearing his presence in Corinth was causing more pain than good, he decided to abandon those plans.

Most likely, though, it was during his previous (and final) visit to Corinth that he wrote his colossal letter to the *Romans*. Paul was a Roman citizen, remember. Therefore, he naturally felt drawn to wanting to visit the big city sometime and meet up with Christian believers that he knew were already there.

In time he'd get his wish.

But it wasn't going to go the way he hoped it would.

All you need to know for now, though, is that Romans is the largest single container of Paul's gospel theology in the New Testament. He lays it out with all the brilliance of his legal training and reasoning skills. Sort of a *magnum opus*, if you will. That's Latin. And sometimes I jump out of my native language and into Latin, because it's how I read my Bible and talk to my kids, who are also fluent in Greek and Pig Latin—OH, MY GOSH, I DID IT AGAIN. I didn't even *mean* to. It's just a spiritual gift.

Seriously, though—get to know the book of Romans, and you'll get to know a lot about what God has done for you through Christ and how it translates into your everyday life.

But all this soaring literature that Paul wrote? All these letters that God inspired as Scripture? Don't be tempted to think he wrote them from a mountain retreat or a cabin in the woods. As he told the Corinthians in his second letter—the one where he defended his office as an apostle—nowhere was there a safe writing desk.

> Five times I received at the hands of the Jews the forty lashes less one. Three times I was beaten with rods. Once I was stoned. Three times I was shipwrecked; a night and a day I was adrift at sea; on frequent journeys, in danger from rivers, danger from robbers, danger from my own people, danger from Gentiles, danger in the city, danger in the wilderness, danger at sea, danger from false brothers; in toil and hardship, through many a sleepless night, in hunger and thirst, often without food, in cold and exposure. And, apart from other things, there is the daily pressure on me of my anxiety for all the churches. (2 Cor. 11:24–28)

Sounds like he could've benefitted from, if nothing else, a better travel agent at least. Unfortunately, the worst was yet to come. Back in Jerusalem after his lengthy third journey, the Jews grabbed him from the temple one day and physically dragged him out, beating him with the intention of killing him. Roman officials intervened, leading to a long, drawn-out battle in the courts over what to do with this guy. The Jews thought they should be able to deal with him however they wanted. But as a citizen of Rome, Paul demanded that his appeal be heard all the way to the top . . . to the emperor himself, if necessary. This Jewish/Roman thing is so complicated. *STUFF SHE KNOWS!* (That was a *Clueless* reference, in case you didn't catch it.)

That's why the long voyage under arrest happened, as well as the shipwreck, his eventual arrival in Rome, and his confinement while awaiting trial. But even then, even there, Paul never stopped thinking about the health and strength and problems and persecutions of believers a world away. Even while imprisoned in Rome, he kept writing letters to the churches:

- *Ephesians*—wisdom and practical advice for Christians living in the world
- *Philippians*—encouragement to rejoice, no matter the circumstances
- *Colossians*—again, how the gospel has freed us from the law

Bear his location in mind next time you're reading from any of these three New Testament books: Ephesians, Philippians, Colossians. Read them through the lens of someone who's stuck behind bars. And ask yourself, like I ask myself, if you'd be able or even interested in writing with this kind of courage, on these kinds of truths, under those kinds of circumstances.

Paul loved him some Jesus. And he was devoted to the people who loved Jesus with him. He loved, loved, loved the church.

Why?

Well, just think about it. In Paul's first encounter with Jesus, Jesus didn't say, "Why are you persecuting the church?" or "Why are you persecuting my people?" He said, "Why are you persecuting *me*?" Jesus so identified with the church that he considered it *his own flesh* (which is why the church is often called "the body of Christ"). And after being changed by Jesus, Paul followed suit.

So, the next time someone tells you they'll take Jesus, but the church they could do without, now you know that the two can't really be separated. Jesus won't do without his church. Neither would Paul, and neither should any of us. The church is who Christ died for—including me and you. If Jesus was that committed to his people, and if Paul was this set on starting and ministering to churches in their moments of need, shouldn't we assume there's no way we can do without the church?

PAUL'S LETTERS TO INDIVIDUALS

Still, not only did Paul write letters that he hoped would circulate among first-century churches; he also wrote to specific individuals sometimes. It's obvious he was the ultimate pen pal.

All four of these particular New Testament letters bore a Roman postmark, most of them probably sent from prison.

Philemon is considered the earliest. Paul wrote this short letter to a wealthy Gentile who apparently had believed in Christ during one of Paul's mission trips. The reason this friend had come to mind again is because Paul, in God's providence, while in Rome, had encountered a man named Onesimus, who turned out to be a runaway slave from Philemon's household.

Now it's only fair to warn you that Paul didn't write his old friend to directly challenge his slaveholding practice.

Slavery was common around the world during this era in history. And while Scripture certainly isn't a champion of slavery—in fact, it condemns slave trading as immoral (1 Tim. 1:10)—the stories of the Bible do reflect the real-world times in which they were written. Early Christians knew they couldn't change entire structures of culture all at once, though they were vigilant in taking one step at a time to see change happen.

But let's read between the lines here and recognize Paul's biblical appeal to human dignity and equality. He had talked Onesimus into going back, fulfilling his duty, and choosing not to live as a fugitive anymore. Paul was now telling Philemon that when Onesimus got back home, he expected things to be different. He wanted Philemon to treat Onesimus as "more than a bondservant, as a beloved brother" (v. 16), as being one with him in the family of Christ. This flows from Paul's own theology—he saw himself as a slave of Christ as well as a brother, co-heir, and friend of Christ as well. He was applying that same framework to a real-life, real-time situation between Philemon and Onesimus.

So in reality, when set against its historical context, Paul's letter to Philemon represents an uncommon statement of brotherhood, and gives us a peek into Paul's heart. He loved Onesimus like a son. This former slave had value to Paul as a friend. That's why he could say to Philemon, "Receive him as you would receive me"—as an equal—and "if he has wronged you at all, or owes you anything, charge that to my account" (vv. 17–18).

The year after Paul wrote Philemon, he wrote to his dear friend Timothy, who was serving as the pastor of the church in Ephesus. This letter is filled with Paul's advice to him on being a godly young man and faithfully shepherding his flock. Like the next two letters that fill out Paul's part of the New Testament, *1 Timothy* remains invaluable to pastors today, as well as to anyone seeking to understand how to handle different church situations in biblical ways.

Titus was another minister of the gospel that Paul had mentored. He was pastoring believers on the island of Crete, a church that was experiencing a lot of struggle. Paul talked with him about the kinds of qualities to look for in choosing good leaders, basically saying that those who claim to be true believers in Christ had better have the actions to back it up.

And now we come to the letter of Paul that pulls on my heart the most. He was in prison at this time, too, and age had caught up with him. He was no longer the young man Jesus had first spoken to. But his blindness had been turned to sight long enough for Paul to know that there was no other way to live, and no other way to die. In fact, although the Bible doesn't say, many scholars believe Nero ordered Paul's execution shortly afterward.

Second Timothy contains his dying words.

Times like these are why I am so excited you've stuck with me for this long. You and I never have to open our Bibles to books like 2 Timothy ever again and read them as if they're detached and free-floating. They're not just nice words of Scripture anymore. They're planted in real time. They're written by people we know. They're connected to everything else the Bible contains in a divinely woven patchwork that never shows age and never wears thin. If anything, its colors and its consistency stand out to us more vividly today than they did before.

So although 2 Timothy may seem like just another few pages hidden in the Bible, remember as you read it that it's the closest thing we have to Paul's last will and testament.

"Do your best to come before winter," he asked his friend (2 Tim. 4:21). It's unlikely, though, Paul made it to winter or that they ever saw each other again. Yet with the shadow of death hanging over him, not even the frailty of Paul's hand or the dimness of his eyes could stifle his passion for the Christ who died to allow us to live.

Paul suffered, yes. But he never wavered, because he was more certain of God than the very table he used when writing his letters. And he implored people to live from the same unwavering faith regardless of their situations or surroundings.

Hear his words, my friend—spoken from the pit of a prison cell, well aware he had few words left to offer: "But I am not ashamed, for I know whom I have believed, and I am convinced that he is able to guard until that day what has been entrusted to me" (2 Tim. 1:12).

Sit here with me, just for a moment.

You'll be closing the pages of this book soon, but the only reason I could write it is because there's another book that never ends. Never wavers. Never fails to meet us where we are. Never leaves us hopeless or alone. Hear the words of Paul as he nears the end of his time on earth:

> I have fought the good fight, I have finished the race, I have kept the faith. Henceforth there is laid up for me the crown of righteousness, which the Lord, the righteous judge, will award to me on that day, and not only to me but also to all who have loved his appearing. (2 Tim. 4:7–8)

Words spoken by a true man of God, echoing through time to reach us exactly where we are.

Chapter 14

THE BIG FINISH

 I've left myself just enough room to fully explain for you the book of Revelation. If you are counting the number of lies I have told, I would appreciate you not mentioning them in your Amazon review.

Frankly, Revelation freaks me out a wee bit. That's why I've brought over into this closing chapter a small handful of other books for us to end with, or maybe I've done it just to keep all the horses and beasts and angels and flying creatures (and me) company. It's intense and detailed and I know it's all true, but it's just not a coloring book I would order. So let's head over to James first and see what he's got to say.

JAMES

You may not have noticed, but we actually had a James-sighting in the previous chapter, when I mentioned that the James of Acts 15, leader of the church in Jerusalem, was author of this later book that bears his name as well as one of Jesus' biological brothers. *Half*-brother, since they didn't share the same father obviously, but he was a child of Mary just the same. And here's the thing you may not have realized. James may not have believed in Jesus (as in, being the Son of God) while Jesus was alive. But he became a devout follower in the wake of Christ's resurrection.

James wrote his letter to "the twelve tribes in the Dispersion" (James 1:1), meaning, Jewish Christians who'd headed out or were driven out as the temperature of religious pressure had grown hot in Jerusalem. "Dispersion" is a modern take on the more classic term *Diaspora,* the scattering of believers out of Palestine "to the end of the earth" (Acts 1:8). But what it cost in inconvenience, the Diaspora more than made up for in Great Commission connotations, because it relocated Christian believers all over the world. They were forced out by efforts to squelch the gospel, but instead, the gospel just traveled all the more quickly to surrounding areas as these believers carried it with them everywhere they went!

James packed the five chapters of his book with practical instruction. It reads like a New Testament version of Proverbs. He tells us to stay joyful when bad things happen, to not be such control freaks over our own schedules and future, to guard against all forms of worldliness, and—most convicting of all—to watch what we say. The tongue is such a small piece of our anatomy, he said, and yet, man, what a firestorm it can whip up.

Basically, he challenges us to be "doers of the word, and not hearers only" (James 1:22). And he questions how someone can claim to have faith in Christ if their lives don't look a whole lot different from everyone else's: "Faith by itself, if it does not have works, is dead" (James 2:17).

Plenty of people have debated how we should interpret James's line of thinking here. Is he saying we're required to *do* stuff in order to be saved, when the whole point of the gospel is that "a person is not justified by works of the law but through faith in Jesus Christ" (Gal. 2:16)?

It's a good question. Because, yes, Christ has done everything required to redeem us and declare us righteous before God, without any of our help at all. "Apart from me," Jesus said, "you can do nothing" (John 15:5). The only thing you and I contributed to what he did on the cross was our sins.

And yet a changed life *should* generate ample evidence to support who we profess to be. As Jesus said, you can tell a tree by its fruit. Or, as James himself said, "Show me your faith apart from your works, and I will show you my faith by my works" (James 2:18).

Both ways of looking at it are true, aren't they really? We can't do anything to earn salvation, but being saved should change what we do. Anybody who's wanting to invest the least possible effort into Christian living ought to seriously wonder if they're the Christian they think they are. We don't *have* to be obedient to him; we *get* to be obedient to him; we're finally *free* to be obedient to him. And we should want our obedience operating at full production all the time.

Thanks for your wise words to us, James.

1 AND 2 PETER

I love Peter, by the way. He is one of my favorites. Back in the Gospels, when he was traipsing around with Jesus, he was always kind of fumbling around with his words, putting his foot in his mouth. His impulsiveness often made him look like an impatient kid.

But he matured. He became more of an elder statesman. He was fully supportive of Paul's mission to evangelize the Gentiles while Peter pursued his own calling of preaching Christ among the Jews. They were complementary pieces in shared mission. I'm not saying the two of them never had a spat or disagreement, but, hey, that's what can happen in close families, even with people we dearly love. And Peter, writing as an older man, referred to Paul as a "beloved brother" (2 Pet. 3:15). They'd been through a lot, these two, and they'd come out furiously united.

Peter's two letters were addressed, as you'd expect, to Jewish Christians scattered around the known world, though I'd like to think some of this Jew/Gentile distinction had begun to dissipate by then, and believers were feeling more united in faith and purpose. The most dominant theme in 1 Peter is perseverance through suffering, which Christians were increasingly undergoing at the hands of the Roman government. And when two people are being mistreated by a common enemy, they tend to form new bonds of alliance.

Life for a first-century Christian was hard. Sometimes seemingly unbearable. But remember, as Peter told them, you have "an inheritance that is imperishable, undefiled, and unfading, kept in heaven for you" (1 Pet. 1:4). So be strong, he said. Hold on to each other. And hold tight to your joy, "so that the tested genuineness of your faith—more precious than gold that perishes though it is tested by fire—may be found to result in praise and glory and honor at the revelation of Jesus Christ" (v. 7).

A couple of years later he wrote 2 Peter, a letter mostly of warning against false prophets and scoffing critics. "Take care that you are not carried away with the error of lawless people and lose your own stability. But grow in the grace and knowledge of our Lord and Savior Jesus Christ. To him be the glory both now and to the day of eternity. Amen" (2 Pet. 3:17–18).

Yes, amen.

HEBREWS

The most curious thing about the book of Hebrews is that nobody really knows who wrote it. Some think it was Paul. It definitely has some "Paul"-sounding passages. But if he did write it, he didn't identify himself anywhere in the letter, which would seem an odd departure from the norm. Others wonder if it might have been authored by Barnabas, still others by Timothy.

Bottom line: who knows? But it's a big, powerhouse piece of writing, no matter who did it.

It's thirteen chapters long, so it doesn't easily condense into a short summary. But much of what the writer of Hebrews sought to communicate was that Jesus is the fulfillment of Old Testament Scripture—that the law, the temple, the priesthood, the sacrifices were all just period pieces. God's intention for them all along was that only in Christ would these things find their fullest, greatest, ultimate expression. Jesus and his new covenant with the people of God are superior to everything that came before.

Hebrews is probably best known for its star-studded eleventh chapter—the so-called "Hall of Faith," lined with quick sketches of men and women throughout biblical history who exercised their faith in God's promises. But the biggest takeaway from this letter is that, in comparison to the priests of old, we now have in Jesus a high priest "who is seated at the right hand of the throne of the Majesty in heaven" (Heb. 8:1)—"one who in every respect has been tempted as we are, yet without sin. Let us then with confidence draw near to the throne of grace, that we may receive mercy and find grace to help in time of need" (Heb. 4:15–16).

Amen again.

JUDE

The book of Jude is an easily overlooked little book in the way back of your Bible. Like Philemon, it's only the length of one chapter, just a couple of dozen verses. And like 2 Peter, its objective is to warn believers about being on guard against people whose teaching sounds like the truth but really isn't the truth.

Most interesting, though, is that like James, Jude was also a brother of Jesus who probably didn't begin believing the gospel until after Jesus had died. I just wonder if at some point Mary got sick of telling them the story of her miraculous conception and the fact that Jesus never got an A- because he was, in fact, the actual Son of God.

Anyway, the most memorable stretch of Jude's letter is the benediction at the end, sort of a stirring doxology: "Now to him who is able to keep you from stumbling and to present you blameless before the presence of the glory with great joy, to the only God, our Savior, through Jesus Christ our Lord, be glory, majesty, dominion, and authority, before all time and now and forever. Amen" (vv. 24–25). Amen and amen.

1, 2, AND 3 JOHN

Coming to these final letters, I'm reminded of how many times I've heard people tell new believers, who typically don't know much about the Bible yet, to start off by reading the Gospel of John. I mean, you know how much I love, love, love the way John captured Christ's life, so I wholeheartedly agree. It's an ideal place to start falling in love with Jesus and his Word.

But I think of a young Christian who takes that advice, and who comes to the end of John's Gospel excited, eager, and hungry for more, wondering where they should go next in their Bible reading. And, man, I'd love being the first to tell them, "Well, hey, did you know John wrote some *other* books in the Bible?" It'd be like having a movie you love or an artist whose music you really enjoy, and then finding out they've released several other things that you've never seen or heard. You couldn't wait to dig a little deeper into their catalog.

Well, here's some additional material from John, all cued up for you.

Once again, he writes in such a unique, personal style that, even when he's warning you to beware the antichrist or something, you still kind of want to have him over for coffee. It's not that he's a pushover, don't get me wrong. He just has such a deep affection for Christ and for the church that it never leaves his tone of voice.

I also love how he often addressed his readers as "little children." He's like a loving, caring dad, protective of his kids, this beloved disciple of Jesus.

It's so, so good to hear from him again.

And just think: all these letters—from John, from Paul, from Peter, and from new friends as well—we get to keep them treasured by our bedside where we can always reach for them, unfold them, smooth them out, and read and reread them again. Like love letters from a sweetheart, they never seem to lose their interest and intrigue. The words they say never change, and yet they speak something more, something new somehow, every time we trace our finger across them.

NEVER ENDING

I'm not sure what's making me more hesitant to write this last part: my reluctance to see you go, or my lack of confidence that I can capture the book of Revelation in just a few paragraphs. I'm not really afraid of it. I totally trust John when he says, "Blessed is the one who reads aloud the words of this prophecy, and blessed are those who hear" (Rev. 1:3). John would never want me to feel anything but loved. And, much more surely, I trust my dear Lord Jesus, who appears so beautifully in the opening chapter, his face "like the sun shining in full strength" (v. 16).

Revelation is just different, is all.

It's almost certainly the last book of the Bible that was written, likely in the late AD 90s. John was an old man by then. All the other apostles were dead; each one martyred, we believe. John alone had survived, but he'd lately been banished to a remote island as punishment for preaching the gospel. And he knew as he languished there on the island of Patmos that all his friends who remained—fellow believers around the world—were also currently suffering persecution under the Romans and their wild imagination for cruelty.

So while the visions contained in this "Revelation to John," as your Bible probably calls it, are definitely an apocalyptic prophecy of the end times, remember to read them through the eyes of John's original audience. Try not to treat the Revelation so much as a puzzle for how to "pin the tail on the antichrist." Be careful about getting way too specific with the prophetic imagery or going crazy trying to chart prospective dates on the end-of-the-world calendar.

Because, look, Jesus is coming back. That's all that really matters. And not only is he coming back to win the ultimate battle and prove himself victor over hell and the grave; he is The Victor already. Satan's doom is already sewn up. Our triumphant Lord, when he returns—as promised, as he predicted—will take his place on a throne that he already occupies today. It's *our* experience that will be different. All this brokenness will be made whole, never to be broken again, in a new heaven and a new earth.

And I think that's mainly what Jesus was wanting to communicate through John. A message of hope; a reason to persevere. These hurting, suffering believers could afford to remain faithful through persecution, even to the death. The reward that didn't often seem worth the pain was as sure as the sunrise. And it still is.

God wins. Evil loses.

> "The kingdom of the world has become the
> kingdom of our Lord and of his Christ, and
> he shall reign forever and ever." (Rev. 11:15)

We are the bride of the Most High, and he is coming back for us. We will live with him in the resurrection for-ever, in a place where sin and suffering are no longer the way of things—where God ushers us into a city of paradise even better than the garden we started with.

It is as certain as the starry night and as beautiful as the lifted veil.

And it's all made possible because of this story we've witnessed—the story of how God in his love continued seeking us as his lost and sinful people, refusing to let our sins be the death of us. Choosing instead to be life for us. That's the thread. God's pursuing love. Irresistible. Unstoppable. A story of rebellion that he gracefully transformed (and continues to transform) into a story of redemption.

I can't think of anything more fitting to end this journey we've taken together than the words of John, as he did his best to do the same. Thank you for walking these roads with me. But it isn't really goodbye. The story continues to weave itself together, giving us every breath we have on earth and an eternity with our Father. We don't know when he will return, but even so, we believe it will be. And because of that, we lift our words and our lives to the God who came to love us in spite of us.

The story goes on and on, and your name, praise the Lord, is written in the margins of every page. Because of that, we say with confidence . . .

Come, Lord Jesus!
The grace of the Lord Jesus be with you all.
Amen.

NOTES

1. Anne Lamott, *Hallelujah Anyway* (New York: Riverhead Books, 2017), 11.

2. A. W. Tozer, *The Knowledge of the Holy* (New York: HarperCollins, 1978), 1.

3. R. C. Sproul, *The Holiness of God* (Carol Stream, IL: Tyndale, 1998), 124.

4. "Hyksos," *Encyclopedia Britannica Online,* s. v. (cited February 6, 2015), http://www.britannica.com/EBchecked/topic/279251/Hyksos.

also available from
ANGIE SMITH

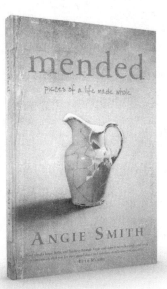

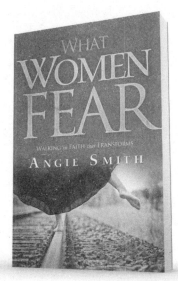

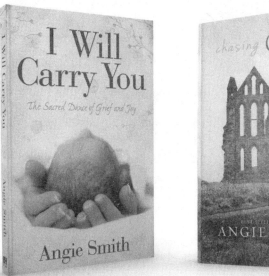

for KIDS

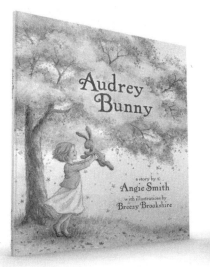

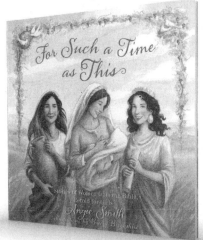

Bible Studies